Roy Hudd's
Huddlines Annual

Based on the award-winning BBC Radio 2 series

Roy Hudd's Huddlines Annual

compiled by

Tony Hare

By arrangement with BBC Enterprises Limited

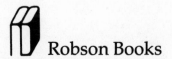

Robson Books

First published in Great Britain in 1994 by Robson Books Ltd, Bolsover House, 5-6
Clipstone Street, London W1P 7EB

Compilation copyright © 1994 Tony Hare
The right of Tony Hare to be identified as author of this work has been asserted by
him in accordance with the Copyright, Designs and Patents Act 1988

Book design by Harold King
Stop Press illustrations by John Jensen
British Library Cataloguing in Publication Data
A catalogue record for this title is available from the British Library

ISBN 0 86051 933 3

Typeset by Harrington & Co., London
Printed in Great Britain by Butler & Tanner Ltd., London and Frome

Contents

FOREWORD I
Hello Happy Huddliners ...

... or, as the honeymooning Huddliner said to his new bride on discovering her standing up in a hammock – 'How?'. This is Big Chief Huddy welcoming you to this year's sooper-dooper *Huddlines Annual*. Our BIG VALUE book has, as usual, all the features and favourites you good boys and girls enjoy so much: 'The Adventures of Knobby the Naturist', 'What Katy did – all the time' and 'Rupert Bare' – they're all here. This time, however, I've done away with all the things that I know, from your crayon-written notes, you *don't* like. Therefore, no skool, no Shakespierre and no pureed vegetables but more, MANY MORE top-heavy ladies and lower-heavy lads *and* more readers' Mums photographs!

This time we're featuring even more of your own work – and here's the BIG news: if your letter or joke appears in this ENORMOUS VALUE almanac you will receive a *genuine* photocopied fiver! And those writers who lean ever so slightly towards the abbey will get a sixer!

Our yardstick for inclusion is simple: If it's lewd we love it; if it's filthy it's funnier; and if it's politically incorrect it's perfect! One word of warning – always try to be fair to the subjects of your disembowelling unless they are politicians, royals, foreigners or anyone who has the slightest distortion of feature, speech, height, thickness or gait. Many entries are rejected because of the use of phrases like 'Be fair' or 'He's a nice man' or 'She's a good woman'. In the world of *Huddlines* there is NO ROOM for deviant views like these. As my maternal grandmother always said, 'GIVE ME A LARGE ONE', and you can't say much fairer than that.

Now, BLACKMAIL is an ugly word. Well, it is to some, but to us Huddliners it can be sweet music. I look at it this way – hmm very nice – but enough of my peccadilloes, let me explain.

MUMMIES and DADDIES are, I know, pesky critters, but they do have more money than you and it should be EVERY HUDDLINER'S DUTY to part them from it. A good way is to MAKE THEM BUY THIS BOOK. It isn't hard to persuade them: if you REALLY TRY you can discover all sorts of little things about your parents – certainly enough to ensure they BUY THIS BOOK. If Mummy is bending over the dustbin, try 'goosing' her. If her reaction is 'Two pints please, milkman' she's either playing Dame in pantomime or she has a secret. Likewise, if you discover a pair of industrial-strength see-through panties in the glove compartment of Daddy's car (and you can if you put them there), just shout, 'Oh look! A surprise for Mummy, Daddy – shall I call her? This sort of blackmail is A-OK. Follow the opening gambit with 'A *Huddlines Annual* will shut my mouth in no time'. Got it? – Good.

Of course, several copies of the Good Old Annual will seal your lips, and my pension fund, forever and Mummy and Daddy will have a good supply to give away as Christmas presents.

Now there's a thought! EVERYONE would like a whizzbang brill *Huddlines Annual* for Christmas. Think of the happiness you, or preferably your parents, can bring by a multi-distribution of THE BEST BOOK EVER?

Imagine the comfort the Royals would derive from a thumb through our carefully crafted kicks in the groin; the shrieks of delight that will issue from the nation's pseuds as they are culled by our totally biased bludgeons. And think of the joyful, childish laughter that will tinkle through the crack in the front door of Number Ten as the PM (pausing only to privatize gold, frankincense and myrrh and hoick up the wise men's salaries) discovers, through these pages, what a caution he is.

Huddliners, it is your SWORN DUTY to upset as many people as you can this Christmas and beyond.

So, finally, THE FOREWORD.

The four words that will show to the world what an idiot ... I mean what a TRUE FRIEND of the BUMPER BOOK you really are. These secret *four words*, if said loudly, clearly and OFTEN to your local bookseller, will bring GREAT HAPPINESS to Old Man Robson, Tony Hare and ME –

'A *Huddlines Annual*, please!'

FOREWORD II

by GLADYS BOWES-LYON

*(Semi-pro percussionist and proprietress of the Ipswich
All-Night Woolshop)*

When Robson Books asked me to write this piece for the *Huddlines Annual*, I really didn't know where to begin. For a start, I've never heard *The News Huddlines* as I only listen to Radio 3, I can't abide Roy Hudd and those stupid antics from that Emu of his, and who's Tony Hare? Unless he's that nice, if overweight, man who comes into my shop twice a week for his three-ply. He's knitting himself a garage and has only got the automatic flip-up door to do before he can cast off.

Let me tell you a little about myself. I was born in 1911, the only daughter of a large family, in a small Suffolk market town called Charvering-in-the-Fields. My father had six mouths to feed, two under his nose, one on his left cheek and the other three round the back of his head. Being the sole female in the family (my mother was a hermaphrodite) I had to run the household on my own, my father having joined a travelling circus as The Man With Twelve Lips.

I was educated at the Martin Boorma . . .

It was at this point that Gladys Bowes-Lyon tragically died, not having finished the Foreword (II). Tony Hare takes over . . .

Putting this book together is a great honour and a labour of love for me. As we go to press I am clocking up my fourteenth year as a writer for *The News Huddlines* and I've enjoyed every minute of it – except the weeks when my sketch 'hit the floor' and I lost my repeat fee.

What a joy it is to work with the likes of Roy Hudd, a man with an even bigger gap in his teeth than mine; June Whitfield, known in the business as The Queen of Standing in Front of a Microphone and Reading a Script – a rather long-winded accolade which she rarely refers to; and, of course, Chris Emmett, The man of a Couple of Voices. I mustn't forget the Band under the direction of the very tall Peter Moss. Then there's a bespectacled jacket which comes in every week and does animal impressions and the announcements. Answers to the name of Richard Clegg, I believe.

On the programme I've worked with several producers, many of whom have gone on to greater things in television – and none of whom have employed me since. Thanks, guys! Having said that, I'm most impressed with the current man at the helm, patronizing brown-noser that I am. Phil Bowker, a most affable Scouser, joined the programme straight from a crèche (am I getting older or are they getting younger?) and is destined to become er . . . another of the producers who once worked on the *Huddlines*.

Choosing the material for the *Huddlines Annual* was no easy task. I had to sift through dozens of scripts – for which I thank fellow writer, Gerry Goddin who had the foresight to save them when others like me chuck 'em away after the show – before making the final selection. Many that didn't quite make it between these pages failed, not because they weren't funny, but because they performed better than they read. For example, Roy's classic Oriental character is hilarious and the writers feed him with excellent lines, but a lot of the humour stems from the over-the-top performance and the juxtaposition of the letter R for the letter L and vice-versa. Doesn't mean much in cold print, but in front of the microphone – that's another story.

Finally, I'd like to thank my colleagues for giving me permission to reproduce their material with little financial reward (just the kudos) and I make no apology for the inclusion of rather more of my own sketches than those of my chums. Nothing to do with self-indulgence, more a question of economics.

I do hope you enjoy this book, but please don't read it while driving a car. For scuba divers a waterproof version is available by sending a Stamped Addressed Oilskin Envelope and coins (not paper money) to Robson Books.

Tony Hare

ACKNOWLEDGEMENTS

These are the people I'd like to (or feel I ought to) mention:

THE PRODUCERS
John Lloyd, Alan Nixon, Jonathan James-Moore, Paul Spencer, Mark Robson, Dirk Maggs (who *has* given me work since), Richard Wilson and . . . oh, I've already given Phil Bowker a name-check.

THE WRITERS
They have been thanked in Foreword II and are credited for their material (so you'll know who to blame), but I would like to convey my gratitude to Charlie Adams for allowing me to insert Mr Friggins – I think I'll rephrase that – for allowing me to *include* Mr Friggins, that perfectly disgusting man Charlie created all those years ago and still gives Chris Emmett great pleasure (and I'm not rephrasing that!).

THE PERFORMERS
Roy, June and Chris. Thanks for the fun every Thursday, for the wonderful characterizations you bring to life from our written words, for your continued friendship and . . . oh, Christ! Let's get on with the bloody book!

A PROFILE ON SOME OF THE HUDDLINES CHARACTERS

MR FRIGGINS

Born Mephisto Friggins, 1932, in Dorset, dishevelled and unwashed, the only son of the Reverend Gaylord Friggins and his wife, Bunty – herself a tireless social reformer. Unfortunately, she failed to reform her wayward offspring who, following an unsavoury incident involving an Akela, a boy soprano and a packet of boiled sweets, swiftly plunged into the abyss of degradation.

Frequently seen in the company of ex-Huddline writer, Charlie Adams (who vehemently denies any association with the man), he enjoys the open countryside, lurking in hedgerows, armed with his binoculars, a tape measure and raincoat velcroed at the front. He has a spare at home, velcroed at the back in case of emergencies.

THUNDERTHIGHS

A formidable woman is Amelia Thunderthighs, whose voice has been likened to that of Edith Evans on Ecstasy. She is a rather enigmatic creature – living in a rambling house in a suburb of Melton Mowbray. We tried to obtain further information about Ms Thunderthighs, but, unfortunately, the house was rambling so much we couldn't get any sense out of it. She has been spotted from time to time in The Gingham Parlour, in the company of a young male model, enjoying a pot of tea and a raspberry lagoon.

JOHN MAJOR

The less said about him, the better.

NORMA MAJOR

Ditto. (For 'him' substitute 'her'.)

THE WRINKLIES

They come in various guises, but are basically stereotypical of the average over-eighty-year-old cantankerous, incontinent, toothless, doddery old codger.

The female of the species frequently displays her below-the-knee heavy-duty directoires, usually as a result of inadvertently tucking her just-above-the-ankle woollen second-hand skirt down the back of them.

We have it on good authority that at least one of her male counterparts has a predilection for wearing a similar undergarment (he says for central heating purposes, but we suspect that the brushed Dralon has a quality not entirely lacking in the erotic when making contact with the bare skin).

ASSORTED OFFICERS OF THE LAW

Be they Superintendents, Inspectors, Sergeants, Constables or WPCs, they are, of course, officious, regimental, amoral, totally unsympathetic, thick, brutal, corrupt and humourless – totally unlike our *real* police who do a splendid and difficult job against impossible odds.

THE ROYAL FAMILY

Gawd bless 'em all – even the mentally deranged ones (if there are any). Some *Huddlines* listeners are quite shocked to hear the Queen Mother sounding like a cross between Irene Handl and Mrs Bridges from *Upstairs, Downstairs* and claim these characteristics bear little resemblance to the serene, majestic lady we all love. But, it has to be said that we only ever see her public image. The Queen Mother has just as much right to behave differently in the privacy of her own surroundings as we have in ours.

THE KINNOCKS

Hooray! Long may they reign in Europe!

REAR-ADMIRAL SIR FRANCIS LIMPET

Bears an uncanny resemblance both in looks and voice to one Major Denis Bloodnok, though is apparently not related. He is a complete buffoon, but a heavily decorated one.

ROGER THRUST

The Midlands' answer to Alan Whicker, though never gets to the exotic places the 'guvnor' goes to. Is a closet member of The Bert Kaempfert Fan Club.

MR and MRS NOTTIDGE

The ultimate 'anoraks'. If they weren't weather enthusiasts they'd be trainspotters. They sound identical in speech, communicating in strange strangulated voices. Secretly, they share each other's clothes.

The other characters are too numerous to profile here. It is up to you, the reader, to let your imagination run riot. If the warped writers can do it, so can you!

A man is worried that his pet Rottweiler might be gay.

Funny, I had an electric eel once that was AC/DC.

Gerry Goddin

The man in black who brings chocolates to the woman in TV commercials is practising some new and difficult stunts.

One of them is how to get the cellophane wrapper off the box.

Tony Wheatley

KAISER RAH, SERA

by Michael Dines

The Queen and hubby, Phil, visit Germany and are are staying at a Guest House: 'Dun Goosestepping'.

CHARACTERS

HM The Queen and HM The Queen Mother . . . JUNE WHITFIELD
Prince Philip . . . ROY HUDD
German Bellboy . . . CHRIS EMMETT

SOUND FX:	*We hear a door open*
BELLBOY:	*(Coming into room)* Unt dis, Herr Prince unt Frau Queen ist your sleeping quarters. Please to haf no smoking on the four-poster, nein cooking in the room and strictly verboten are das ladies-in-waiting after 10 o'clock.
PHILIP:	What! Have to bally do I suppose – I hate these confounded bed and banquet places.
QUEEN:	One's sure it will be very comfortable. Don't complain, Philip – after all, we're only in Germany for five days.
BELLBOY:	Ach, das kaputten British economy – you couldn't afford the full week? So, I vill the suitcases put down ...
SOUND FX:	*Bellboy dropping a large number of varying-sized suitcases on floor*
BELLBOY:	*(Breathless)* Unt I vill the rest bring up in ein minute. Danke. Danke? *(Coughs)* Danke!
QUEEN:	Philip! Tip!

PHILIP: Eh? Errr, a tenner should do. Here y'are and, just to show who y'talking to, look at that picture on it.

BELLBOY: Vat is das? Ach! Velcome, Mr Charles Dickens – I am not recognizing you without the beard.

PHILIP: What? Other side, y'bally fool – sketch of her indoors in her working clothes.

BELLBOY: Mein Gott! Englisher ten pounds – the last time I am seeing something worth this much, it was in the mouth of der Andrex puppy. Have you no proper cash – Francs, Deutschmarks, ERM money?

QUEEN: We prefer ER II money, thank you . . .

PHILIP: Even if the exchange rate for our nickers does go up and down faster than Madonna's. It's all the fault of your confounded bunch of Bundesbankers.

QUEEN: *(Starts unpacking)* Philip! We found the president very charming when he shook our hand.

PHILIP: Hope y'counted y'fingers afterwards. Y'can't trust Johnny foreigner, if you ask me.

BELLBOY: Pardon mein herr, is this your passport on the floor? Mr Philip Schleswig-Holstein-Sonderburg-Glücksburg, Prince of Greece and Denmark . . .

PHILIP: *(Coughs embarrassedly)* Keep meaning to get that bally thing changed. Right, er, want a hand unpackin', dear? What're you looking for – the lightweight travel crown?

QUEEN: One is trying to find our schedule, we jotted some ideas on it. Check those trunks over there, will you? We know we have to take a symbolic walk through the Brandenburg gate.

PHILIP: Just remember the foreign country code and shut it after you.

QUEEN: And we're visiting East Germany.

BELLBOY: Jah, is very rundown, massive unemployment – years of bad government.

PHILIP: If we wanted to see that we could've stayed at home. What else?

QUEEN: Then we're having a ride on a London double-decker bus, one *is* looking forward to that – we so enjoy it when they say 'Only One On Top'. Then there's our staggered arrival times in Berlin, Dresden, Potsdam . . .

PHILIP: We'll be staggering all over the place. Who organized this confounded trip – y'sister Margaret? Waste of bally time.

QUEEN: Philip, we're here because the British government is trying to become more popular with the Germans.

PHILIP: You'd think the British government'd try and become more popular with the British. What's Germany got that we haven't?

BELLBOY: Ein unified country? Also the sound money, fine lagers, unt here the sauerkraut is very popular.

PHILIP: Is she? Well y'can have Princess Michael back any time y'like.

QUEEN: Oh, we can't find our schedule in these cases, one had better check the others downstairs. *(As she exits)* And Philip, do remind me to pick up one of those clocks that are like Charles – you know, cuckoo.

SOUND FX: *Door closes*

PHILIP: I'll just finish unpacking these bally trunks – going to give me a hand?

BELLBOY: Oh, jah – all people with German blood are workaholics.

PHILIP: Really? I'd better check Edward's birth certificate then. Let me see – morning dress, evening dress, dinner suit, elevenses suit . . . what's this in the corner? Looks like an abandoned tourist map – all pink, mauve and crumpled . . .

BELLBOY: I will straighten it for you, Herr Prince – in das trouser press, extra steam . . .

17

QUEEN MUM: Ow! Oh, oof, oh gor 'blige me! Get off, you Boschey bellboy! Almost put a sprain on the international relations there.

PHILIP: Queen ma-in-law! What are you doing in my trunk – stowing away?

QUEEN MUM: 'Corst not – I took a wrong turning in Buck House looking for the gin cellar and, afore I knewed it, this door shut and I was being given a thorough raffling by them Thiefrow Boggage handlers. Nice to be back abroad though.

BELLBOY: You haf been to Europe before?

QUEEN MUM: Hoh yus, dear! Mind you, it's not like years ago – Mussolini stirring up Italy, them Khazis marching through Germany and Winston Churchill telling the government what to do . . . well, p'raps it *is* like years ago. I remembers me and Bertie come here for a holiday – afore his brother run off with that Barnes Wallace Simpson, the one with the big bouncers.

PHILIP: You had a trip to Germany?

QUEEN MUM: All the time, dear. We went rumbling through the Slack Forest, Bertie wore them leather shorts – with a special pocket for his beef jerky – and I had the bob-tailed boots. Ooh it was fun, me whistling the Hippy Wanderer and Bertie stopping and getting me to hold his knapsack while he had a quick yodel at every clump of fir. 'Corst, when that Hair Hitlist got all unnecessary over his living room, we had to stay home, so's we could hammer the Hun.

BELLBOY: Donner und Blitzen! You are talking of the children of mein Fatherland.

QUEEN MUM: Well, he never married your Motherland, dear. Ho yus, we went through six years of rationing, blackout and blitz. Wasn't all fun though – we had that Vera Lynn as well. Anyways, that's all behind us now, must be going. Help me under the table, Philocrates. I's got to tunnel me way out.

PHILIP: What? You're tunnelling back to Blighty?

QUEEN MUM: 'Corst not, dear – while I'm on vocation, I's going to them El
               Alamo celebrations . . . *(Going off)* it'll be the only bit of sand
               without a German beach towel on it . . .

               (She exits)

SOUND FX: *Door opens and closes*

BELLBOY: Mein Gott – is all your family like her? I see of your Fergie suing
               ein photographer for two and a half million unt saying she will
               give das money to charity.

PHILIP: Yes – the bally Home for Fallen Duchesses, I expect.

SOUND FX: *Door opens*

QUEEN: *(Entering room)* Philip! We have remembered what we were
               going to do to make Britain more popular with the Germans. We
               have offered to rename one of our establishments for them.

PHILIP: What! We're going to call Buck House the Buckstaag, or have
               Sandringham Schloss?

BELLBOY: Perhaps change your royal name to a German one?

QUEEN: Don't be silly, we can't change back this soon. No, we are letting
               them rename something they already control, and it should do
               wonders for the value of our money.

PHILIP: Eh? Oh, I see. Bally good idea. So next time we need some
               confounded travellers' cheques . . .

QUEEN: Precisely – we can get them from the Bundesbank of England.

STOP PRESS

BBC2 showed four hours of gay programmes last Saturday night.

It had a huge audience — people were too frightened to turn over.

Gerry Goddin

STOP PRESS

Exchange and Mart is now carrying wife-swapping ads.

Yes, you can now get one with one previous owner, a good body but needs servicing regularly.

Tony Farrer

GOING STRAIGHT

by Tony Hare

CHARACTERS

Doris Kumquat . . . CHRIS EMMETT

Superintendent . . . ROY HUDD

Sergeant Grunt . . . JUNE WHITFIELD

Inspector Everard . . . CHRIS EMMETT as Larry Grayson

The scene is a corner greengrocer's shop. The owner is examining his damsons for bruises when the door opens with a tinkle and an officious- looking type wearing raincoat and trilby enters. The shopkeeper looks up and greets his customer.

SHOPKEEPER: Good morning, sir – can I help you?

SUPER: *(Officiously)* Are you Mr Doris Kumquat – owner of this establishment?

SHOPKEEPER: That is correct.

SUPER: And are all these fruit and vegetable comestibles under your jurisdiction?

SHOPKEEPER: Yes, they are. I have the best Coxes in the neighbourhood.

SUPER: How plural of you. And how well endowed are you in the Cucumber Department?

SHOPKEEPER: Pardon?

21

SUPER:	I shall put it another way. Do you have any cucumbers in your stocks?
SHOPKEEPER:	Oh, yes – plenty. There. Cop a load of that.
	(He slaps cucumber on the counter)
SUPER:	Aha! Just as I thought! *(He produces a police whistle from pocket and gives a short blast on it, then calls)* Fiona! In here, if you please!
	(The door opens and a policewoman enters)
POLICEWOMAN:	You blasted, sir?
SUPER:	Indeed I did. We've got another one.
SHOPKEEPER:	Excuse me – what's going on?
SUPER:	All in good time. I, sir, am a representative from the European Commission – namely Superintendent Danvers Delight of the Vegetable Police, Cucumber Division – and this is my assistant, Sergeant Fiona Grunt of Lengths and Girths.
POLICEWOMAN:	That is I – and you're nicked, sunbeam.
SHOPKEEPER:	Nicked? What for?
SUPER:	For being in possession of a bent one.
SHOPKEEPER:	*(Incredulously)* That is no business of yours.
SUPER:	Oh, but it is. Under new EC regulations you are in possession of a number of cucumbers with curved proclivities.
SHOPKEEPER:	You're joking!
SUPER:	Oh, would that I was, sir. Tell him, Sergeant Grunt.
POLICEWOMAN:	Section 34B, Paragraph 18 of the EC ruling on cucumber

curvature clearly states that there must be no more than 10 millimetres of arc per length of 10 centimetres.

SUPER: Beautifully expounded, Fiona.

POLICEWOMAN: Thanks, Super.

SUPER: Now get out your protractors.

POLICEWOMAN: Certainly, sir.

(The air is rent asunder by the sound of a zip and two loud pops as Sergeant Grunt produces her protractors. She turns to her boss)

POLICEWOMAN: *And* the tape measure?

SUPER: Why not? Let's go for the big one.

(A tape measure is subsequently produced and extended)

POLICEWOMAN: No doubt about it, Super. This gargantuan gherkin is way beyond the agreed EC limit.

SUPER: Are you saying the item in question is not upright, Sergeant Grunt?

POLICEWOMAN: Upright? This is not so much a cucumber as a green boomerang with pips.

SUPER: Got him! Are you in for it now, sunshine.

SHOPKEEPER: This is preposterous!

SUPER: Latin, eh? Well, I know it as a cucumber. This gelatinous objet d'art of an emerald hue is positively deformed and as a representative of Her Majesty's Vegetable Police, I am arresting you.

SHOPKEEPER: Hang on – you can't arrest me. On a technicality.

SUPER: What? Explain yourself!

SHOPKEEPER: Well, according to the same EC regulations, the cucumber is not a vegetable – it's classified as a fruit. Only the Fruit Police can charge me.

SUPER: Curses! I can't abide barrack room lawyers.

(Mr Kumquat is dragged behind some shelves, from behind which is heard a thump, followed by a squelching sound)

SHOPKEEPER: *(An agonized yell)* Owwwwww! Right in the Victorias!

SUPER: There was no call for that, Fiona – especially with a theodolite.

POLICEWOMAN: Sorry, Super – I can't stand barrack room lawyers either.

SUPER: You won't wriggle out of this one, sunshine. We're ahead of you there. Even as we speak, the Fruit Squad is hot on our heels.

(As if on cue, the shop doorbell tinkles and another officer, looking remarkably like Larry Grayson, enters, light-footedly)

POLICEWOMAN: 'Morning, Inspector.

SUPER: If you'll permit me to handle your cucumber for a moment, Mr Kumquat .. there – what do you think of that, Inspector Everard?

INSPECTOR: Well, hey ho! Wait till WPC Slack Alice sees this one! She'll water at the mouth. Come to think of it, I'm dribbling myself!

STOP PRESS

A 64 year old woman has just retired after 50 years of making 10 million Cornish Pasties.

She said, originally she was only meant to be filling in.

Gerry Goddin

WASH AND GROW
by **Oleh Stepaniuk**

Voice-over: JUNE WHITFIELD

SOUND FX	*Changing room atmosphere*
VOICE-OVER:	Spend time on shampoo *and* conditioner. . . ?
SOUND FX:	*Locker door slams*
VOICE-OVER:	Take two bottles into the shower. . . ?
SOUND FX:	*Locker door slams*
VOICE-OVER:	Not me!
SOUND FX:	*Locker door slams*
VOICE-OVER:	Because I'm the girl who used to star in the Sellafield Guided Tour advert and now I'm bald as a coot.

OLD BOY NETWORK
by Richard Stoneman

The scene is the restaurant of an old-fashioned type Gentlemen's Club.

CHARACTERS

Tuffty, a very posh old fogey . . . ROY HUDD in a grey wig and moustache

Buffty, another very posh old fogey . . . CHRIS EMMETT in a grey wig, moustache and monocle

Chief Executive, a very posh woman . . . JUNE WHITFIELD in grey wig, no moustache (well, just a hint)

Club Waiter . . . RICHARD CLEGG, *Huddlines* Announcer in waiter's costume (ill-fitting)

TUFFTY:	*(Calls out)* I say, Buffty – over here!
BUFFTY:	*(Approaching)* Ah, Tuffty – there you are. Might have guessed you'd nab the best table in the club for our little lunch.
TUFFTY:	I had to pull rank.
BUFFTY:	Did you? Well, you always enjoyed a bit of rank–pulling I seem to remember. Wasn't that why you were kicked out of Eton in 1929?
TUFFTY:	That's right – caught with the pretty boy from the cadet force. But let's not bring that up again.
BUFFTY:	Not what you said at the time, ha ha. . . .

TUFFTY:	Oh do shut up, Buffty. Why did you want to see me anyway?
BUFFTY:	Well, you know I've been with some merchant bankers?
TUFFTY:	I had heard that, yes.
BUFFTY:	They tell me that a new chief executive is about to be appointed at Loopers de Zoot Holdings plc.
TUFFTY:	Loopers de Zoot Holdings? Never heard of them.
BUFFTY:	Oh, pity.
TUFFTY:	Why?
BUFFTY:	You're their chairman.
TUFFTY:	Am I? Oh, you mean the place I'm taken every Thursday for a chinwag with some chaps I met at Oxford?
BUFFTY:	That's it – they're your board of directors.
TUFFTY:	What – Fluffty, Guffty, Muffty, Chuffty and Luffty?
BUFFTY:	And Kevin.
TUFFTY:	Yes. I'm still not sure about grammar school boys.
BUFFTY:	Got to move with the times, old chap. And that's why I wanted you to meet your new chief executive before the next board meeting.
TUFFTY:	You've asked him to join us for lunch?
BUFFTY:	Yes. But I ought to warn you. . . .

(They are interrupted by the arrival of the new chief executive, a posh yet dynamic female)

C. EXEC.:	Good afternoon, gentlemen.

TUFFTY:	Good God! It's a woo. . . a wooo. . .
C.EXEC.:	Go on, say it. I'm a woman.
TUFFTY:	A wooo. . . No, I'm sorry – I just can't get my tongue round it.
BUFFTY:	Some things never change.
C.EXEC.:	May I join you?
TUFFTY:	No, dammit – you may not! This is a gentlemen's club, run for gentlemen by gentlemen.
WAITER:	*(Very soft and effeminate)* Ready to order, sirs, madam?
TUFFTY:	*(Under breath)* And some of the men are *very* gentle. *(Normal)* Come back in a minute – will you, Clary?
WAITER:	*(Going off)* Very good, sir.
BUFFTY:	Wasn't he your fag at Eton?
TUFFTY:	That was a vicious rumour put around by that little bitch in the cadet force.
C. EXEC.:	Gentlemen, please may we get down to business? As the prospective chief executive of Loopers de Zoot I must warn you I'll want changes. For a start. . .
TUFFTY:	Just a second, young lady. I think you're assuming too much. There's not a man in the company who'll work for a girlie. And I'm one of them.
C. EXEC.:	Oh? Can't you imagine being under a woman?
TUFFTY:	Well, given prior notice – yes. But let's stick to business, shall we?
C. EXEC.:	Very well. I have to work with you as my chairman, so will I have your support?
TUFFTY:	I'm afraid not. Women are too sissy, they have babies twice a

year and suffer from pre-prandial tension every week. Besides, you weren't at the same school as me.

BUFFTY: Ah, now Tuffty does have a point there. The reason we chaps in the city get along so well is that we all know each other's quirks.

TUFFTY: Usually just by their first names, but we do know them.

C. EXEC.: So if I could prove a close association with you, you'd be quite happy to have me as chief executive?

TUFFTY: Yes – if we've got something in common, I'd grasp your bosom to mine like a long-lost matron. Come to think of it, you do look slightly familiar.

C. EXEC.: I should do. Take a look at this bit of paper and I'll order lunch to celebrate my appointment.

TUFFTY: Good Lord!

BUFFTY: What is it – proof that she's the Eton cadet with a sex change?

TUFFTY: Something far stranger than that.

C. EXEC.: It's a certificate which makes the job mine.

BUFFTY: What!

TUFFTY: I thought she seemed familiar, Buffty. Apparently, I married her in 1957.

STOP PRESS

A man who had a vasectomy said that when he feels a bit frisky his hair stands on end.

So when women meet him they say: "Are you raising your hat or are you just pleased to see me?"

Tony Wheatley

STOP PRESS

Vegetarians want to ban egg and spoon races because they're cruel to chickens.

I suppose it depends on where you put the spoon, really.

Tony Farrer

STOP PRESS

To make her lips look sexier, Madonna is having injections made from cows' tails.

Even if it doesn't work, at least it'll keep the flies off her face.

Gerry Goddin

FLYING FOGIES

by **Stuart Silver**

A seventy-five-year-old pensioner hit the news a while back when she started taking flying lessons. Well, she got fed up waiting for the council to repair her lift. But the question the Huddlines wanted to know was, where do pensioner pilots go to get their wings? Is there a special school for the Sanatogen Set? The investigative team followed the exploits of one such elderly couple (played by Roy Hudd and June Whitfield) under the guidance of their instructor, the equally elderly Chris Emmett.

AMY   Can you see the the control tower yet, Icarus?

ICARUS: Yes, Amy. Keep going and hold on to your stick . . . OK – left a bit . . . right a bit . . . now!

SOUND FX: *Knocking on door. It opens*

INSTRUCTOR: Hello. Welcome to Saga Flying School, the Sour-away Day Centre for the senile. I'm the Air Commode-ore.

AMY: Don't you mean commodore?

INSTRUCTOR: No – I'm not as young as I used to be. Now then, why do you want to learn to fly?

ICARUS: Our budgie just died.

AMY: And it's a shame to waste his perch.

INSTRUCTOR: Ah, but flying ain't that easy. Do you know what it's like to have the wind whistling past your ears as you struggle to regain control?

ICARUS: Yers – but I'm getting a new nightshirt for Christmas.

AMY: In the war they used to call him 'Hurricane'.

INSTRUCTOR: I can't imagine why.

AMY: Well, he was in a terrible dog-fight once.

INSTRUCTOR: Really?

ICARUS: Yers – a gang of chihuahuas tried to grab me Winalot rations . . .

SOUND FX: *Jets roar past in turn at high speed*

AMY: Cooor! What was that?

INSTRUCTOR: Our answer to the RAF's Red Arrows . . . the Green Strainers display team.

ICARUS: Here – look, Amy! Vertical take-off walk frames. Can we have a go?

INSTRUCTOR: No. You can't do any real flying 'til we've taught you how to handle sub-zero temperatures at high altitudes.

AMY: How d'you do that then?

INSTRUCTOR: We move you into a top-floor council flat. We used to try taking people up in our special pensioner airbus, but nobody ever got on.

ICARUS: Why not?

INSTRUCTOR: Cos the conductor kept ringing the bell before we had a chance. Now, over here is our mock-up old codger's cockpit. As you can see, the pensioner pilot seat has three positions: Upright, Tilted and Golden Wedding Anniversary.

AMY: Cooo! Can I try it out?

INSTRUCTOR: Not until you've passed the initiative test.

ICARUS: Don't you worry, mush – she might be seventy-five but she's got the mind of a ninety-year-old.

32

INSTRUCTOR:	We'll soon see. Imagine you're flying a party of pensioners on a long trip. What's the first thing you do?
AMY:	Hand round the fruit bonbons.
INSTRUCTOR:	Correct. Then, suddenly, you look down at your equipment and you've only got five thousand feet left. What do you do?
ICARUS:	Ring the chiropodist.
INSTRUCTOR:	Aha! But what does a pensioner pilot use to ring the chiropodist?
AMY:	My grandson.
INSTRUCTOR:	Correct! But now, what's this? You're going into a dive . . .
ICARUS:	D'you mean that little cinema in Soho?
INSTRUCTOR:	Shtum! And now the throbbing starts.
ICARUS:	You *do* mean that little cinema in Soho!
INSTRUCTOR:	No! The plane's in trouble. So you have to get all the pensioners out. It's cold in the sea and nobody's wearing their industrial-strength Damarts. What do you do to keep warm?
ICARUS:	Break out the Ralgex.
INSTRUCTOR:	Wrong! A pensioner pilot opens *this* to keep warm.
SOUND FX*:*	*Inflating raft*
ICARUS:	Cooor! It's an inflatable public library!
INSTRUCTOR:	Yers – and the air inside is conditioned by a dosser who sits in the corner and pongs.
AMY:	Well, Air Commode-ore – did we pass?
INSTRUCTOR:	Pass?! As far as I'm concerned, you don't know what day it is

33

and you're the most senile pair of old duffers I've ever met.

ICARUS: So?

INSTRUCTOR: I'm recommending you both as Air Traffic Controllers.

ICARUS/AMY: Whoopeeee!

The Queen has invited
Captain Mark Phillips for the
Royal Christmas.

Well, that's their turkey
sorted out, then.

Oleh Stepaniuk

CHIMNEY SWEEPS
by **Gerry Goddin**

Two chimney sweeps are leaving the conference room at a hotel. One of them is doubled up with pain. At first his colleague seems oblivious to this.

1ST SWEEP: *(Yorkshire)* Eee, lad – that were a good conference, wurn it?

2ND SWEEP: *(In pain)* By heck it were!

1ST SWEEP: *(Proudly)* Just think – that's the first national conference of Chimney Sweeps to be held in t' wurld. Doan it make yur glow inside?

2ND SWEEP: *(Strained)* By gum, it does that.

1ST SWEEP: What's wrong with thee, lad? Thou's dosna seem keen about it.

2ND SWEEP: Wur that cloakroom attendant a chimney sweep too?

1ST SWEEP: 'Course he were. Why does thee ask?

2ND SWEEP: *(In agony)* Well, that's the last bloody time I ask him for a wash and brush up!

PUPPET THEATRE

by Julian Dutton

Characters

Roger Thrust, a 'Brummie' Reporter – CHRIS EMMETT
Punch and Judy man – ROY HUDD

SOUND FX:	*Seaside atmosphere (waves, seagulls, crowds, etc)*
ROGER:	Hello! This week I've been sent to Bournemouth, where the Dorset Festival of Arts and Crafts is well and truly under way. And one of the highlights of this magnificent flowering of British culture is, of course – Ebeneezer Flip and his amazing Punch and Judy Show. Good afternoon, Mr Flip.
MR FLIP:	Good afternoon, there!
ROGER:	Now, Mr Flip – your show is no ordinary Punch and Judy Show, is it?
MR FLIP:	Good gracious no! No – instead of the usual Punch and Judy story, I present a vast repertoire of classic plays drawn from twenty centuries of world drama.
ROGER:	Amazing. So, what have you got for us first?
MR FLIP:	*Uncle Vanya* by Chekhov.
ROGER:	Remarkable. So, here then, for the first time on a Punch and Judy stage, Chekhov's *Uncle Vanya*, performed by Ebeneezer Flip and Company.

MR FLIP:	Ahem! *(As Punch)* You stupid crocodile! You've eaten all the sausages! Take that!
SOUND FX:	*Thwack of stick*
MR FLIP:	*(As Crocodile)* Ow! *(As Punch)* That's the way to do it! That's the way to do it!
	(Uncomfortable pause)
ROGER:	Is that it?
MR FLIP:	That is it – yes.
ROGER:	Mmm. Bit short – isn't it, Mr Flip?
MR FLIP:	Ah, well – that was just the two-act version.
ROGER:	I see. Correct me if I'm wrong, Mr Flip – but I can't recall *Uncle Vanya* having a crocodile in it who eats sausages.
MR FLIP:	No, well you see, in Chekhov's version the crocodile's a very minor character.
ROGER:	Oh really?
MR FLIP:	Yes. In fact, he's so minor he's never even mentioned. So I thought for my version I'd build up his part a bit.
ROGER:	I see. And the sausages?
MR FLIP:	Ah yes. Now some people don't think that sausages crop up a lot in *Uncle Vanya*.
ROGER:	No?
MR FLIP:	No. But I beg to differ. If you look closely, you'll find that behind each dramatic twist in the tale lurks a chipolata.
ROGER:	Indeed. And what have you got for us next, Mr Flip?
MR FLIP:	*King Lear* by William Shakespeare.

ROGER: Marvellous. In your own time, then. *King Lear* by William
                Shakespeare.

MR FLIP: Thank you. Ahem. *(As Punch)* You stupid crocodile! You've
                eaten all the sausages! Take that!

SOUND FX: *Thwack of stick*

MR FLIP: *(As Crocodile)* Ow! *(As Punch)* That's the way to do it!
                That's the way to do it!

                (Uncomfortable pause)

ROGER: Mmm. Run me round the Bullring if I'm wrong on this, Mr
                Flip, but wasn't that a mite similar to the Chekhov?

MR FLIP: How dare you! Anyone can see that the Chekhov embodies a
                gentle stoicism qualified by the ennobling effect of human
                action: while the *King Lear* – especially in Acts Two and
                Three – represents an almost Jacobean echo of the fatalism of
                Sophocles, or even Seneca in his darker moments.

ROGER: Quite. And, of course, the sausages cropped up again, didn't
                they?

MR FLIP: Ah. You noticed. Well, you see, in my version, King Lear
                isn't reconciled with his daughter, who then dies . . .

ROGER: No?

MR FLIP: No. He's reconciled with his pet crocodile, who then eats a
                sausage.

ROGER: Indeed . . . Mr Flip, do any of your classic versions of world
                drama not have sausages or crocodiles in them?

MR FLIP: Oooh, let me see . . . There's the *Two Sausages of Verona*.
                That's definitely got sausages in. Um . . . *An Inspector Calls –
                and brings a Sausage. Hamlet – Crocodile of Denmark* . . .

ROGER: Crocodile of Denmark?!

MR FLIP:	*(Proudly)* That's one of mine.
ROGER:	Hamlet wasn't a crocodile!
MR FLIP:	Prove it.
ROGER:	What?
MR FLIP:	*(Emphatically)* Show me one line in that entire play that says Hamlet hasn't got dirty great fangs and a ten-foot green tail.
ROGER:	Well, I . . .
MR FLIP:	Exactly. Then there's that great classic of twentieth-century comedy: *No Sex Please, I'm a Pork and Beef Banger.*
ROGER:	You're a fraud – aren't you, Mr Flip?
MR FLIP:	Pardon?
ROGER:	This isn't culture! It's just a rotten old Punch and Judy Show palming itself off as world-class drama!
MR FLIP:	How dare you! My company rivals the RSC !
ROGER:	Rivals the RSC ?! Look at 'em! They're just a couple of lifeless wooden puppets!
MR FLIP:	You fiend! They may well be lifeless and wooden, but that's the very reason my leading actors have been asked to tour the world in the most popular classic of recent years!
ROGER:	What's that – Bernard Shaw? Tom Stoppard?
MR FLIP:	No – the stage version of *Prisoner: Cell Block H*! So there! *(As Mr Punch)* That's the way to do it! That's the way to do it!
SOUND FX:	*Thwack of stick*
ROGER:	Ow!

BARKING UP THE WRONG TREE

by Gerry Goddin

CHARACTERS

Doctor . . . ROY HUDD

Mr Friggins . . . CHRIS EMMETT

A doctor's surgery

SOUND FX*:*	*A knock on door*
DOCTOR:	Come in!
SOUND FX*:*	*Door opening*
FRIGGINS:	'Morning, Doctor!
DOCTOR:	Mr Friggins! What seems to be the trouble *this* week?
FRIGGINS:	Well, doctor – I've been taking that aphrodisiac you gave me made from the bark of an African tree. And when I woke up this morning, this had happened.
SOUND FX:	*Whoosh*
DOCTOR:	Good heavens! It's covered with leaves!
FRIGGINS:	It's murder on a windy day, doctor.
DOCTOR:	I bet it is! Let's have another look.

SOUND FX:	*Whoosh*
DOCTOR:	Is that a bird's nest?
FRIGGINS:	No, doctor.
DOCTOR:	Ah, yes – my mistake. Still, you'd better watch out for woodpeckers. Let's have one last look.
SOUND FX:	*Whoosh*
DOCTOR:	Yes. Mmm. I see. It must be the autumn.
FRIGGINS:	Why do you say that, doctor?
DOCTOR:	Your conkers have dropped off.

****

AVAILABLE SOON!

The Friggins Pop-Up Book (in Hardback)
(Special Limited Edition – Price £29.99)

Also available as a **Paperback Flick-book with Free 3D Glasses**
(Price £9.99)

All orders posted in Plain Brown Envelope and come with a Health Warning.

****

THE HYPNOTIST

by **Tony Farrer**

The scene is a football club changing room. The team manager is addressing his players after a match.

MANAGER: *(Chris)* Well played, lads – you've done Barnet Football Club proud. We've won our first game of the season at last.

PLAYER: *(Roy)* Well, it's all down to you, Boss. Getting that hypnotist to help us was sheer inspiration. Me and the lads have never felt so relaxed in a game.

MANAGER: Yes, well . . . that's what management's all about, son – bringing in the right people to help you when you're struggling.

PLAYER: That's right, Boss. There's only one thing that bothers me though.

MANAGER: What's that?

PLAYER: When does he wake the other team up?

KINNOCK – MISSING IN ACTION

by Tony Hare

When Neil Kinnock was leader of the Labour Party he took a lot of flak from the Tory press – and when he set about a bunch of yobbos who were accosting his daughter, they really went to town, accusing him of using bully boy tactics. The police, on the other hand, approved wholeheartedly. Well, for the purpose of this sketch they did.

BAND: *The* Dragnet *theme – then under**

VOICE-OVER: *(Urgent American)* You've seen *Rambo 12*, *Deathwish 24* and *Terminator 37*. Now – Red Flag Productions proudly brings to your screens a new super-hero – self-appointed vigilante – expert in martial arts and hedge-trimming: Kinnock – The Ginger Ninja! Our story begins down in Police Headquarters at the 43rd Precinct, between the Spud-U-Like and Mr Byrite in Ealing High Street.

BAND: *Theme ends*

SOUND FX:*:* *Knock on door, then it is opened*

KINNOCK: You wanted to see me, Chief – aren't I?

CHIEF: *(English policeman)* Ah, yes – Kinnock. Good of you to come. I'm Inspector Fit-up. We couldn't help but notice the way you handled those young hooligans at the weekend. Most impressive. And, as you know, manpower here at the 43rd Precinct is pretty low, so would you like to help us out?

*THEN UNDER means the sound dips in volume to allow narrative to be heard over it. THEN UP, of course, means volume increases when narration is over.

KINNOCK:	Ooh, lovely, lovely! Eisteddfod.
CHIEF:	We need somebody to clean up the streets of Ealing, get rid of the garbage that passes itself off as the dregs of humanity. It's a jungle out there. So what do you say?
KINNOCK:	I'm your man, boyo. When do I start, look you, isn't it?
CHIEF:	Right away. You'll need extensive training in self-defence, so you'd better prepare your wife for a house-guest. Every spare moment of your day will be spent in perfecting the martial arts. Good luck, Kinnock.
BAND:	Dragnet *theme comes up, then out*
SOUND FX:	*Martial art fight (over-amplified kicks, punches, slaps, bone crunches, smashing furniture, breaking glass, etc). This is accompanied by yells and grunts from Kinnock and his Japanese opponent in combat*
SOUND FX:	*Door opening*
GLENYS:	Neil! *(Kung Fu noises stop)* What *are* you doing? Get down off the mantelpiece at once!
NEIL:	Oh hello, Glenys bach. This is my new Kung Fu instructor.
INSTRUCTOR:	*(Japanese)* Herro! Me Toshiba Hitachi!
GLENYS:	Bless you. Neil – in the kitchen please.
NEIL:	Just a moment, Glenys – I'm practising to become a finely tuned fighting machine, afraid of nothing, guided by my inner karma and answerable to no one.
GLENYS:	*(Sternly)* Neil! Get in that kitchen!
NEIL:	*(Meekly)* Yes, Glenys. Right away. I won't be a moment, Hitachi.
INSTRUCTOR:	Bless you!

(Neil and Glenys go into the kitchen, closing the door behind them)

GLENYS: How long is this silly nonsense going to last?

NEIL: It's not silly nonsense, Glenys – I've been chosen.

GLENYS: Who by – the Ovalteenies?

NEIL: You can scoff, aren't I? But I'm going to make Ealing a cleaner and safer place to live in. Do you know I'm only one grade below a black boot in kick-boxing?

GLENYS: Yes, and look what it's doing to the place! My kitchen cabinet all over the floor in pieces!

NEIL: That wasn't me, Glenys boyo – that's the one we bought from MFI last week. It fell apart when I slammed the door shut.

(With a frenzied yell, Hitachi the instructor comes crashing through the door, splintering wood everywhere)

NEIL: Hitachi – when you want to come in open the door, there's a good chap, don't you?

INSTRUCTOR: Solly! OK, Glasshopper Kinnock – time for final test . . . on your own.

NEIL: Ooh, lovely, lovely!

INSTRUCTOR: Take this – and good luck.

(Sounds of struggling. Karate noises (whooshes), etc while Neil grunts and strains, finally giving up)

NEIL: *(Deflated)* It's no good! I'm a failure! Glenys, can you do it?

GLENYS: Honestly, Neil! Can't you open a simple packet of biscuits?

INSTRUCTOR: No – it is no disglace for Glasshopper Kinnock. Only Peek-

Fleen hold solution to great mystery of unravelling biscuit wrapper.

NEIL: And, Glenys – how many more times must I tell you not to buy ginger nuts. You know how sensitive I am about these things.

GLENYS: Think yourself lucky I didn't buy Garibaldi.

BAND: *Linking music (*Dragnet *theme) up, then under*

VOICE-OVER: *(Urgent American)* And so – a new vigilante is let loose in Ealing and confronts his first adversaries. . .

SOUND FX: *Dustbins kicked, bottles breaking*

OMNES: *(Commotion)*

NEIL: Oh, jow! jow! That's enough! Clear off, you unruly scum, aren't I?

WOMAN OAP: Who says so? You think we're taking orders from you, you Welsh Wuzzock?

MAN OAP: Go on, gal – you tell him!

NEIL: You senior citizen street gangs are all the same, isn't it? You hang around the post office, terrorizing decent people. . .

MAN OAP: We're queuing, mate. You can't move us on.

NEIL: I won't warn you again, boyo.

MAN OAP: Go on, Mabel – I think he needs to be taught a lesson. Give it to him.

WOMAN OAP: All right, freckle-face – chew on this!

NEIL: My God – a fully-loaded automatic pension book! All right – you've forced me to use my ultimate Kung Fu weapon, look you, isn't it?

SOUND FX:	*Zip being undone*
WOMAN OAP:	Arnold! He's whipping out his Dirty Harry!
NEIL:	You're wrong – it's my Dusty Taffy . . . the most lethal of all martial arts weapons.
SOUND FX:	*Whooshes of weapon being brandished in martial arts fashion*
NEIL:	One blow with this will crush every bone in your body.
MAN OAP:	But what is it?
NEIL:	A starched leek. Go ahead, bach – make my day.
SOUND FX:	*Furious fighting (yells, grunts, whooshes, etc)*
BAND:	Dragnet *link*
NARRATOR:	*(Urgent American)* Within a week, the Ealing Post Office was a safer place to cash a Giro, but then a new menace hits the borough. Down at the 43rd Precinct. . .
NEIL:	You sent for me, Chief, didn't they?
INSPECTOR:	Yes, Kinnock – we're very pleased with what you've achieved, but we've got another crisis on our hands. The borough's desperately short of money. I had the Mayor in the office this morning.
NEIL:	I trust you weren't disturbed.
INSPECTOR:	Fortunately, no. He was in a most anxious state . . .
NEIL:	I'm not surprised.
INSPECTOR:	. . . begging us for financial help. But our bribe fund is sacrosanct. So the result is severe cut-backs – and a change of tactics as far as you're concerned.

NEIL:	You mean, you've finished with my services, aren't I?
INSPECTOR:	Oh, good lord, no. We still need you.
NEIL:	To clean up the streets and make Ealing a more respectable place to live?
INSPECTOR:	Right on the button, chummy. You report first thing Monday morning to the Town Hall to collect your broom and dustcart.
NEIL:	Ooh, lovely, lovely!

Tony Wheatley

A QUICKIE

THE BREAKTHROUGH OF THE CHUNNEL

by **Oleh Stepaniuk**

It is the historic occasion when England and France were united for the first time as the two halves of the Channel Tunnel finally met. Much was made of the English achievement, but what about the French point of view?

CHARACTERS

1st French Tunnel Digger . . . ROY HUDD

2nd French Tunnel Digger . . . CHRIS EMMETT

SOUND FX: *Drilling/ heavy plant machinery working*

1ST FRENCHMAN: Zere! An historic moment! At last! After centuries of planning and three years of digging ze Chunnel – Britain and France are now joined.

2ND FRENCHMAN: Mais oui. And with it will come ze inevitable flood of English culture. Like ze Fish and Cheeps.

1ST FRENCHMAN: Ze Chinese takeaway. Ze double-decker.

2ND FRENCHMAN: Ze umbrellas and bowler hats.

1ST FRENCHMAN: Ze English bobby.

2ND FRENCHMAN: Ze Mrs Thatcher. . . .

(A pause)

BOTH: Mon dieu! Quick everyone! Fill it in! Fill it in!

WE ARE NOT AMUSED – YOU CAN'T SEE HER NIPPLES

by Nick Revell

Shock! Horror! It was revealed in some of the tabloids that Queen Victoria once bought a photo of a topless model from a Swedish photographer in Wolverhampton. A likely story! But let's go back in time . . . just in case.

CHARACTERS
Narrator 1 . . . ROY HUDD
Narrator 2 . . . CHRIS EMMETT
Margaret Thatcher . . . JUNE WHITFIELD
Ronald Reagan . . . CHRIS EMMETT
Narrator 3 . . . JUNE WHITFIELD
Cricket Umpire . . . ROY HUDD
Indian Cricketer . . . CHRIS EMMETT
Music Hall MC . . . ROY HUDD

Queen Victoria . . . JUNE WHITFIELD
Prince Albert . . . ROY HUDD
Sven, The Photographer . . . CHRIS EMMETT

NARRATOR 1:   The year is 1857, the heyday of the British Empire. But the working classes see little prosperity as they suffer cruel working practices, starvation wages and child labour. But at least the television was better than it is today.

NARRATOR 2:   Philanthropists and reformers were trying to improve the lot of the poor but were branded as wets and communists by a young Grantham girl, Margaret Roberts, who declares:

THATCHER:	There is no alternative!
NARRATOR 2:	The first ever letter is sent by Penny Post.
NARRATOR 1:	The Post Office say it should arrive any day now. In the United States a young actor declares his ambitions . . .
REAGAN:	Nancy, this Grecian 2000 makes me look years younger. Hell, I look so good one day I could stand for President.
NARRATOR 3:	In the Colonies, the Indian Mutiny is in full swing . . .
SOUND FX:	*Cricket match / ball struck*
CROWD:	Howzat?!
UMPIRE:	Out.
INDIAN PLAYER:	The ball bounced before he caught it. I'm not going.
UMPIRE:	You dare to challenge the authority of the British Umpire?
NARRATOR 3:	Back home, the main source of entertainment was the Music Hall . . .
SOUND FX:	*Music hall. Audience making merry*
MC:	My Lords, Ladies and Gentlemen – I give you the delectably demure . . .
AUDIENCE:	Ooh!
MC:	The immaculate epitome of innocence . . .
AUDIENCE:	Ooh!
MC:	The veritably virginal . . .
AUDIENCE:	Ooh!
MC:	Miss Joan Collins!

NARRATOR 2:	Meanwhile, outside a backstreet photographer's shop in Wolverhampton . . .
SOUND FX:	*Horses' hooves on cobbles*
Q VICTORIA:	Albert?
ALBERT:	Jawohl, mein liebling?
Q VICTORIA:	Do stop that goose-stepping – it makes me nervous. Ah, here we are, 'Sven's Adult Photographic Emporium. Engraving and Plating two shillings'.
ALBERT:	Cheaper than Shepherd Market.
Q VICTORIA:	What?
ALBERT:	Nothing, my little edelweiss. Shall we enter?
SOUND FX:	*Shop door opening with bell tinkle*
PHOTOGRAPHER:	*(A Swedish Brummie)* Good day to you. Welcome to Sven's – Purveyor of Porn to the Posh. What can I do for you?
ALBERT:	I don't like this man, darling.
Q VICTORIA:	Why not?
ALBERT:	His accent is sillier than mine.
Q VICTORIA:	I understand you deal in tasteful and artistic representations of the female form.
PHOTO:	Oh, you want a naked bint? How about these two?
ALBERT:	Mein Gott! Not the kind of thing you'd see in der newspapers, is it?
PHOTO:	No. But you've just given me an idea. *(Shouts)* Messenger boy! Go and tell Mr Murdoch I want to see him. You'll find him at The Blackmailer's Arms. Well, do you want it?

Q VICTORIA: They're . . . it's beautiful. We'll take it.

PHOTO: Here – don't I know you from somewhere? Don't you go down the Pussy Cat A-Go-Go Club on Women Only Nights?

ALBERT: Mein wife is der Queen of England!

PHOTO: Thought I recognized you. By the way, can I ask how you heard about my shop?

Q VICTORIA: Well, last time I was in Scotland John Brown recommended you when he was entertaining me with his magic lantern.

ALBERT: I don't remember that . . .

Q VICTORIA: You wouldn't, darling. You were decorating your Christmas tree at the time.

ALBERT: So, how much are we owing you?

PHOTO: Well, I always like to charge according to how much the girl in the photo is wearing – see?

ALBERT: Ah, yes. So this one will be . . .

PHOTO: You've guessed it. Half a knicker!

(The sketch ends with a goon show-type chord from band – Victorian style)

STOP PRESS

Talking watches are now on sale in the shops

Trouble is, they keep winding each other up all day.

Gerry Goddin

In the New Forest, a totally unmodernised brick and slate building, without sanitation or water, has been sold for £128,000.

It's going to be used as a hospital.

Oleh Stepaniuk

Jokers screwed a man's false teeth to the ceiling of a pub.

He said he was so embarrassed — his feet kept dangling over the bar.

Tony Farrer

DRUNK IN CHARGE

by **Tony Farrer**

A police car has just flagged down an erratically driven vehicle. The copper gets out of his car and approaches the other one. He indicates the driver to wind his window down.

POLICEMAN: *(Roy)* All right, sir – would you mind stepping out of your car? Good grief! I don't need a breathalyser – I can see you're as drunk as a lord.

DRIVER: *(Chris, very drunk)* Junk?! Don't be ridic . . . ridicle . . . stupid ossifer. I've had that brand-new anti-jinking device . . . *(hiccups)* fitted. If I'd had tooooooo much to jink the engine on my Ford Fiesta would cut out.

POLICEMAN: Really. Well, I've got news for you, sir.

DRIVER: What's that, ossifer?

POLICEMAN: You're driving a Mini Metro.

AND NOW THE WEATHER

by Tony Hare

ROGER THRUST: *(The Brummie reporter)* Hello! Well, here I am in Canvey Island – Number 27 Refinery Mews, to be precise – to discuss one of the Englishman's favourite topics . . . the weather. Last Sunday was St Martin's Day, the day tradition tells us determines the weather of the winter to come – and all over the country amateur forecasters have predicted what we're in for during the next few months. With me are two such sages who certainly know their onions . . . (just my little joke) . . . Neville and Brenda Nottidge.

MR NOTTIDGE: *(The Ultimate Male Anorak)* Hello, I'm Brenda.

MRS NOTTIDGE: *(The Ultimate Female Anorak)* And I'm Neville.

ROGER: Now, firstly – let me get one thing straight.

MR NOTTIDGE: Certainly. Wife of mine – avert your eyes. This could be unpleasant.

ROGER: No, no – I merely want to clarify the fact that you call yourselves weather forecasters and not meteorologists.

MR NOTTIDGE: You are quite correct.

ROGER: And why is that?

MRS NOTTIDGE: We can't say meteorologists.

ROGER: So tell me, how *do* you make your predictions?

MR NOTTIDGE: Well, first we check the barometric readings, comparing them to the millibar graph in relation to the hygroscopic charts. . .

MRS NOTTIDGE: Then I go out the back to see if his length of seaweed's gone soggy.

ROGER: Ah well now – isn't that what it's all about? Guesswork? Relying upon ridiculous old wives' tales and folklore?

MR NOTTIDGE: It is no such thing. Why, we have a saying that sums it up perfectly:

> The rains will come tumbling down if
> Granny's surgical stockings go stiff . . .

. . . And it works every time, doesn't it, Neville?

MRS NOTTIDGE: Yes, it does, Brenda. We swear by my mother's surgical stockings. We hung them on the whirligig clothesline last night and sure enough, it rained.

MR NOTTIDGE: And this morning they were as stiff as an ironing board. Took us ages to get her out of them.

MRS NOTTIDGE: But the doctor says the peg marks will fade with time.

ROGER: You expect me to believe such twaddle?

MR NOTTIDGE: He doubts our credulity, Neville.

MRS NOTTIDGE: Then show him your whelk.

ROGER: Pardon?

MR NOTTIDGE: It's like a big winkle.

ROGER: I know what a whelk is. What's that got to do with forecasting weather?

MR &MRS NOTTIDGE: *(Both snort with laughter)*

MRS NOTTIDGE: He's obviously not read our pamphlet: *The Crustacean's Role in Meteorology.*

MR NOTTIDGE: Nor he hasn't. We tried predicting with the aid of a lobster, but it isn't always reliable.

MRS NOTTIDGE: Mind you, the next day there was a definite nip in the air.

MR NOTTIDGE: Oh, very droll, wife of mine. Us weather forecasters do have a sense of humour.

ROGER: You must have if you expect me to believe we owe the changes in our climate to an oversized winkle. You'll be telling me next that thing on your roof is a weather cockle.

MR NOTTIDGE: Do I detect a touch of irony in your voice, sir?

ROGER: And will we be seeing Ian McGaskill telling us to cast not a clout till May is out?

MRS NOTTIDGE: Ah, we have to agree, that little epithet is meaningless. May never goes out.

MR NOTTIDGE: That's the wife's mother, sir.

ROGER: Except when you take her for a spin on your whirligig clothes line.

MR NOTTIDGE: That *was* a mistake. No – very few clouts are cast in this house.

ROGER: I'm pleased to hear it. Now, several of your colleagues have predicted a White Christmas this year.

MR NOTTIDGE: That is quite correct. My bladder is infallible.

ROGER: Your bladder?

MRS NOTTIDGE: Yes, my hubby swears by the pig's bladder hanging in the conservatory.

MR NOTTIDGE: That and the old adage: The Christmas will be white, if the squirrel's nuts are tight.

MRS NOTTIDGE: And the squirrel's hoard is very lean this year.

MR NOTTIDGE: She's very good at cleaning up jokes is my good lady wife.

ROGER: Yes, I've noticed. Well, I'm sorry, but I think this whole thing's a load of old codswallop.

MR NOTTIDGE: Ah, that's the way we predict storms.

ROGER: What is?

MR NOTTIDGE: Walloping old cod.

ROGER: What I mean is, I can't give any credence to the reliability of your methods.

MRS NOTTIDGE: Oh, yes? Was it us who three years ago on that Thursday in October said: 'What gales?'

ROGER: All right, then – perhaps you'd like to show me your operation.

MR NOTTIDGE: Certainly not – the scar is in a most intimate place.

ROGER: I meant, give me a demonstration as to how you come by your predictions.

MR NOTTIDGE: Well, we'd like to very much, but I'm afraid it's not quite convenient at the moment.

MRS NOTTIDGE: No, Brenda has promised to take me out for a picnic in the country.

MR NOTTIDGE: After I've made a quick phone call.

ROGER: A phone call?

MR NOTTIDGE: Yes, the Weatherline. We don't want to go out if there's a chance of rain.

STOP PRESS

A 90 year old madam runs a sex parlour for the over 60s and each session lasts an hour.

Half an hour to undress and half an hour to remember why they're there.

Tony Wheatley

STOP PRESS

A pub landlady has been given eight pot-bellied pigs.

Fancy that— an instant darts team.

Oleh Stepaniuk

THE HUDDLINES ANNUAL

KIDDIES KORNER

RUPERT AND THE MYSTERIOUS FLASHING

by **Michael Dines**

JUNE: This is the tale of Rupert Bear,
Whose TV show made viewers stare,
For when they gave it closer looks,
They saw a pile of dirty books.
So, are his exploits turning funny?

ROY: *(Rupert)* Too flippin' right – I need the money!
. . . Do you know how much a red designer cashmere jumper and yellow mohair trousers cost? Specially for an unemployed bear living at home . . .

JUNE: The story starts when mother asked
Rupert to do a simple task.

SOUND FX: INTERIOR COTTAGE ACOUSTIC. TICKING CLOCK

CHRIS: *(Gruff)* You'll have to go and get the shopping,
Tonight's our evening for wife-swapping,
Here's my purse and shoulder bag . . .

ROY: That wasn't mum, but dad – in drag.

SOUND FX: COUNTRYSIDE ATMOSPHERE, BIRDS ETC

JUNE: Cried Rupert, trudging down the lane:

ROY: Walking to town's a bloody pain,
This journey would be much less fuss if
The Tories hadn't cut the buses.
. . . This could take Shakespeare off the A-Level syllabus, you know . . .

SOUND FX: CITY ATMOSPHERE, HEAVY TRAFFIC. A CAR SCREECHES PAST

JUNE: He turned the corner, gasped, looked glum,

ROY: All of Nutwood's just a slum!

The streets are full of filth and slime,

CHRIS: *(Freddie Fox)* That's thanks to Michael Heseltine.

ROY: It's Freddie Fox! You old twister,
Tell me – how is Sam, your sister?
I remember how she liked to shock us,
By flashing her . . .

CHRIS: . . . Fags, behind the lockers?
Just look around, it seems a pity,
Nutwood's now an inner city,
What we need is a good fairy,

ROY: And all you get's Archbishop Carey.
But tell me, what of our old chums?

CHRIS: They've all ended up as bums.
Bill Badger croaked, a boozy lush,

ROY: And got turned into a shaving brush?
Has anyone seen Edward Trunk?
(We hear an elephant trumpet, off)

CHRIS: He dyed his tusks and went all punk.
And Porky Pig, you know he found a
Dead end job on the bacon counter.
(We hear pig squeals, off)

ROY: What keeps the bailiffs from your door?

CHRIS: Blue books and mags, come see the store.

SOUND FX: SHOP DOOR OPENING WITH BELL TINKLE

JUNE: So Rupert went into the shop,
And out on stalks his eyes did pop.
He saw the book *A Guide To Knickers,*

ROY: A useful buy for naughty vicars.

CHRIS: And here's a snap of Algy pug,

ROY: Stark naked on a fireside rug!
. . . I see the vet hasn't got to him yet . . .

CHRIS: In this box my fav'rite chum is

ROY: A blow-up dolly from Ann Summers.
My word, you have extensive stocks,

(Chains rattle)

And whips, and masks and chains, and locks.
I'd like to stay and learn the ropes,

(Assorted whipcracks, clanks and groans)

JUNE: So Rupert did, and all his hopes
Soon came true, as can be seen

ROY: In this month's Play-Bear Magazine –
. . . *Pity about the staple through me growler though* . . .

JUNE: And the moral is: That being naughty,

ROY: Brings in more cash than a UB40!
*(As he goes off:) Do you like me red and yellow check
stockings and suspenders? Whoar! Gimme a drink,
someone – I'll have a can of Special Bruin. I'm going to
get totally rat-arsed – or should I say: bear-arsed?
Wha-hay!*

THE HUDDLINES BAND PLAYS PUNK VERSION OF 'TEDDY BEARS PICNIC'

NOT ON YOUR NODDY

a short story by **Ged Parsons**

*A publishing company (not this one, I hope) has claimed that
Noddy and Big Ears are too perverted for today's kiddies.
The* Huddlines *researcher dipped into his Mother Goose and,
unable to resist a quick gander, unearthed the latest
adventures of Toytown's favourite inhabitants. We reproduce
the unexpurgated story here.*

One fine morning, Noddy woke up feeling happy. 'Gosh! I'm
feeling happy!' he exclaimed.

'Stop that at once!' cried Happy. 'Oh, my goodness! I'm in
the wrong house . . . the other six dwarfs will be missing
me!' he said. So, with a hop and a skip, he scampered off
. . . very slowly.

'Oh, dear!' thought Noddy. 'Now what shall I do? I know
– I'll go down to the woods!' And with that, he put on his little
red hat and fastened his little dirty raincoat.

'Oh, dear!' he said to himself. 'I forgot to put on my little
blue shorts . . . hur, hur, hur! Never mind!'

And, laughing happily, he skipped outside. He jumped into
his tiny little car, with its tiny little seat, and held the tiny little
steering wheel.

'Oh, dear!' he sighed. 'I wish I'd never bought this Skoda!'

And off he drove. Parp, parp! he went. Parp, parp! No
more curried toadstools for him. He drove on till he met
Prickly Hedgehog.

'Hello, Noddy!' cried Prickly Hedgehog. Splat! went the
tiny little car.

'Tough luck, flat-boy!' cried Noddy. And on he went. Then
he saw a funny little house by the road. It was painted all
sorts of colours and happy laughter could be heard. Sleepy
Bunny sat outside.

'Oi, goofy!!' cried Noddy. 'Is this the gingerbread house?'

'No,' said Sleepy Bunny, sleepily. 'This is the Acid House!'
And he went on nibbling the grass. 'Wow, this is good stuff,
Noddy man . . . far out!'

Just then, Mr Plod the policeman arrived, wielding his truncheon. Thwack! Thwack! went the truncheon.

'Ow! Ouch!' screamed Noddy. 'Stop hitting me!'

'Sorry, Noddy,' said Mr Plod, bringing his knee up into Noddy's wedding tackle. 'Force of habit. Now, is this your car?'

'Of course it is!' said Noddy.

'Then what's the registration number, sunshine?'

'Noddy 1,' said Noddy. 'Can I go now?'

'Not yet, sonny,' said Mr Plod. 'Someone's been stealing cars in Toytown, and I aim to nab him.'

'Why don't you pin the blame on Golly?' said Noddy. 'You usually do.' And off he went with a parp, parp. At last he reached the woods.

'Now for a little walk,' he thought. 'I'll walk and walk, and nod my little head. Hear how the bell on my hat tinkles.'

And, sure enough, the little bell on his hat tinkled.

'Oh, I do so love a little tinkle in the woods!' Noddy ejaculated. Suddenly, he saw something poking at him through the bushes. 'Is that you, Big Ears?' he asked.

'No!' came a gruff voice. 'I'm a reporter from the *People*. I've just taken a photo of you tinkling in the woods – this'll make a great story!'

'No, you can't do that!' cried Noddy. 'My friend Big Ears won't let you!'

'Oh, yeah?' sneered the nasty man. 'And what'll he do?'

Noddy laughed. 'You'll soon see. In fact, here he comes now. Big Ears – do your stuff.'

And, sure enough, out of the bushes stepped Prince Charles, one hand behind his back. With the other he grabbed the nasty reporter by the scruff of his neck.

'Err . . . right!' said Prince Charles. 'First, one will report you to the press council and get you sacked . . .'

Then a furious argument ensued and they all lived noisily ever after.

FLOBBLEDOB

by **Mike Coleman**

The BBC proudly announced that their biggest selling video was 'Watch with Mother' starring The Flowerpot Men, having made over a million pounds in royalties. Who would have thought that a sophisticated modern audience would be interested in two old plonkers spouting gibberish at each other? But that's enough about Saint and Greavsie. The burning question was, how were Bill and Ben handling such fame and success? The Huddlines disguised itself as a bag of manure and hopped down to the end of the garden to eavesdrop . . .

SIGNATURE TUNE: *The Flowerpot Men Theme*

NARRATOR: *(June)* Hello, boys and girls. Down at the end of the long, long garden there's an old potting shed. And in that potting shed, when nobody can see them, two little flowerpot men called Bill and Ben get up to some very naughty games. Let's tear them away from each other and see what they get up to, shall we? Hello, Bill – hello, Ben.

BILL: *(Chris – falsetto)* Aw, flobbledob!

BEN: *(Roy – basso profundo)* Aw, flobbledob!

NARRATOR: Ho, ho – I bet I know what you're going to do with that white powder on the back of your hand, Bill. You're going to throw it at Ben, aren't you?

BILL: Naw, naw, naw . . . powdle sniffleob! *(Sniffs) (Ecstatic)* Aw . . . flobbledobbledob! *(Laughs)*

BEN: High-as-a-kite-a-dobbleob!!

NARRATOR: Now, what's Ben found under the table?

BEN: Flobbledobble fizzy-popple-ob.

NARRATOR: I wonder what's in the bottle. Can you read the label, boys and girls? *(With difficulty)* Dom . . . Perignon – I expect it's some sort of fizzy pop, don't you?

SOUND FX:	*Champagne cork pop*
BEN:	*(Glug, Glug, Glug. Huge belch)*
NARRATOR:	My word! Ben was thirsty – wasn't he, boys and girls?
BEN:	*(Drunk)* Aww, bleebleobble pissed-as-a-fartobble-ob!
NARRATOR:	What are Bill and Ben doing? *(A slight pause)* Bill?
BILL:	*(Actorish)* Sorry, love. I've dried. What's my line again?
BEN:	Aw, flobbledob!
BILL:	Oh, yes – of course. And what's my motivation?
NARRATOR:	Puppets don't have motivation, Bill. Now stop being such a lardy.
BEN:	Aw, flobble-dobble-dobble-obble-fleedle-bobble-ob.
NARRATOR:	And what does that mean, Ben?
BEN:	It means, tell the silly cow we're stars now and we don't have to put up with her patronizing bullsh . . . .
NARRATOR:	Now, just you listen here . . .
BEN:	Aw, flob off!
BILL:	He says . . .
NARRATOR:	Thank you. I don't think you need to translate that. Shall we get on?
BEN:	No, I'm sorry. It's not good enough – I want my character developed. I want a love interest. What about that Weed? She's a nice bit of rampant floribunda, ain't she?
BILL:	Looble flobble wopper flobble!
BEN:	*(Filthy laugh)* You dirty little devil!
NARRATOR:	Look – this is preposterous . . .

BEN:	I warn you, missis – we're all united. Just come back through here.
SOUND FX:	*Door opening – we hear a general commotion going on*
NARRATOR:	Good Lord . . . Andy Pandy, Teddy, The Woodentops, Rag, Tag and Bobtail . . . and what's *he* doing over there?
BEN:	He's Muffin the Mule *(aside:) And the next line's been cut!* Together we make up the Confederation for the Reinstatement of Antiquated Puppetstars – that's C-R-A-P for short. And after the sales of the video, we're all millionaires . . . so you'd better start listening to us. We want star billing . . .
OTHERS:	*(Noisy affirmation)*
BEN:	We want proper adult dialogue with swear words . . .
OTHERS:	*(Noisy affirmation)*
BEN:	And most of all we want *Watch With Mother* reinstated every day on BBC1
OTHERS:	*(Noisy affirmation)*
BEN:	Brothers . . . what do we want?
OTHERS:	Flobbledob flobbledob!!
BEN:	And when do we want it?
OTHERS:	*(High-pitched) Weeeeeeeed!*
NARRATOR:	But there's no way BBC1 will reinstate *Watch with Mother*.
BEN:	What – you mean people don't want to watch wooden puppets any more?
NARRATOR:	No, it's not that. It's just that it's all done so much better by the cast of *Neighbours*.
ALL:	Flobbledob cobbers-dob!

A HUMOROUS BRACE AND BIT ABOUT RICHARD THE THIRDS*

by Tony Hare

CHARACTERS

Bert Dunlittle (A Broad Cockney) . . . ROY HUDD
Elsie, His Wife (A Broad Cockney) . . . JUNE WHITFIELD
Gielgud, The Butler (OTT Sir John) . . . CHRIS EMMETT

ROY'S LINK: I was in the pub the other evening, having a quiet pint when all of a sudden I saw this bloke at the bar give another bloke a Gorbals Kiss. Well, I nearly choked on me Crème de Menthe shandy. Gorbals Kiss? That's a head-butt, according to the latest edition of *Brewer's Dictionary of Twentieth Century Phrase and Fable.* But with all these new euphemisms entering our language, I wonder how it will affect those masters of the Queen's English – the Cockney.

Let's go over to the palace of self-made whelk-baron and full-time Pearly King, His Majesty Bert Dunlittle and his good lady wife, Queen Elsie, to find out . . .

SOUND FX: *Bow bells pealing loudly, then cut off suddenly*

BERT: *(Really over-the-top Cockney)* Gor luvaduck! I'm getting rid of that alarm clock, Else, me old trouble and strife – it's too noisy.

* *A humorous skit about words.*

70

ELSE:	*(Also OTT Cockney)* Nah, Bert – me cock sparrer! 'S the only thing that gets you up in the morning', innit? Gaw blimey!
BERT:	Yeah, strike a light! I don't know why we employ a butler – *he's* the ice cream freezer who's s'posed to wake us . . . wiv our breakfast – strap up an' no mistake.
ELSE:	Stone the flippin' crows – you're right, me old china . . .
BERT:	Else?
ELSE:	Yeah, Bert?
BERT:	Why are we talking like this? There ain't no tourists around now.
ELSE:	I should flippin' hope not – we're still in our Uncle Ned.
SOUND FX:	*Knock on door*
BERT:	Come in!
SOUND FX:	*Door opening*
GIELGUD:	Ahhh! Good morning, sir – ma'rm! Your breakfasts! A plate of Jack the Rippers, boned as you like them.
BERT:	Abaht time too, Gielgud – what kept yer, eh John?
GIELGUD:	A thousand apologies, sir – I've been running your Jeremy Beadle.
BERT:	'Ere! Watch your bleedin' language in front of the carvin' knife 'ere.
ELSE:	Yeah – what kind of talk is that then? That ain't real Cockney.
GIELGUD:	Your observations are truly devastating, ma'rm.
BERT:	'Ere – are you takin' the Sir Arthur Bliss?

71

ELSE: That ain't real Cockney neither, Bert – an' no mistake.

BERT: All right – don't you puff and dart! I curse the day that flippin' *Brewer's Dictionary* ever came out with its poncy new meanings. Well, Gielgud – I'm still waiting to find out what running my Jeremy Beadle means.

GIELGUD: I would have thought it was painfully obvious, sir. Jeremy Beadle . . . *Game For a Laugh* . . . bahf! I'm running your bahf – as you people would have it. I trust that clarifies things.

BERT: Well, I'll be blowed!

GIELGUD: I'm sure you will, sir. May I assist you in your dressing?

BERT: No, you may not! *(Painfully)* Gordon Bennett! Elsie, 'ow many more times must I tell yer – don't sew the pearl buttons on the *inside* of me underpants!

ELSE: As long as you're pearly king, you'll 'ave buttons sewn on everyfink . . . including your soldier ants.

BERT: Gor, blige me – she's at it now! That book's gotta go!

GIELGUD: Sir, if I might interject – may I say that's a nasty-looking Hampton you've got there.

BERT: You what?

GIELGUD: Have you tried putting a mustard poultice on it?

ELSE: 'Ere – wha's 'e rabbitin' on abaht, Bert?

GIELGUD: The master's Hampton Court Maze. That nasty-looking *graze* . . . on his knee.

BERT: That does it! I want that book out of this cat and mouse right away! I'm not 'aving my butler gettin' a touch of the Brewer's.

GIELGUD: That is one problem I have never suffered from, sir.

BERT:	I'm talking about the dictionary!
SOUND FX:	*Door chimes (they play 'Boiled Beef and Carrots')*
GIELGUD:	Ah, that'll be your son – young Jay Arthur.
ELSE:	Which one is he? We've got so many saucepan lids I lose count of 'oo's 'oo. 'Old up – is he the ginger one?
GIELGUD:	He *is* the one with the red hair, yes.
BERT:	'Alf a tick – you ain't lettin' 'im in 'ere – 'e's the one 'oo advised me to buy shares in Thames TV. Gor, dear oh lor! Call 'i'self a merchant banker?
GIELGUD:	At last, sir!
BERT:	At last what, John?
GIELGUD:	Some Cockney rhyming slang we're *all* agreed about!

STOP PRESS

In a test by "Which" magazine, Heinz Baked Beans came last.

Blimey - I hope it doesn't backfire on them.

Gerry Goddin

CAR-FUL AS YOU GO
by Nick R. Thomas

Two joyriders, played by Roy and Chris, have just broken into a car. The driver starts the engine.

JOYRIDER 1:   Well, that was pretty easy – wasn't it, mate?

JOYRIDER 2:   Yeah – I love this joyriding lark, don't you? 'Ere, hang on a minute . . .

SOUND FX: *Phut. Engine conks out*

JOYRIDER 1:   What's happening?

JOYRIDER 2:   I dunno – the engine's just cut out.

JOYRIDER 1:   And all the doors are jammed. You know what this means?

JOYRIDER 2:   Yeah – we've been caught by one of them new booby-trapped cars planted by the police.

JOYRIDER 1:   No – we've just nicked a Skoda.

CENTRE-FOREWORD

by Chris Emmett

It's a great thrill to be represented
in this book, even though the
reader has been deprived
of my brilliant voice
characterisationz (both of them).
Never mind, perhapz this will
become one of thoze talking
books on cassette, then I'll have
a chance to shine through —
unless my part is read by
Tony Slattery.
Please excuze the crayon but
Matron won't allow us sharp
objects in here.
Chriz Emmett

THANKS FOR THE MEMORY

by **Tony Hare**

CHARACTERS

MC . . . ROY HUDD
Prompter . . . CHRIS EMMETT
Prunella . . . JUNE WHITFIELD
Bernie . . . ROY HUDD
Reggie . . . CHRIS EMMETT
Dorian . . . CHRIS EMMETT
Desmond . . . ROY HUDD
Hermoine . . . JUNE WHITFIELD

OMNES:	*(General hubbub)*
SOUND FX:	*Blowing into microphone*
MC:	Hello! Can I have your attention, please? Firstly, may I welcome you to this, the very first World Memory Championship – or Memoriad, as we like to call it. My name is . . . er . . . There! I had it on the tip of my tongue – now it's gone. What a silly narner. Ah . . . ! Silly Billy? That's it! My name's William Narner and I'm the . . . er . . .
PROMPTER:	*(Loud whisper)* MC!
MC:	Thank you. MC for this . . . er . . .
PROMPTER:	*(Loud whisper)* Evening!
MC:	Good evening. Firstly, may I welcome you to . . .

PROMPTER: *(Loud whisper)* You've done that bit!

MC: Have I? Well, anyway – your names will be called out
             when we require you on stage to demonstrate your
             powers. In the meantime, why don't you get to know one
             another over a nice cup of . . . um . . . that hot brown stuff.
             Good luck, everybody.

(Meanwhile, in the green room the contestants are waiting their turn . . .)

PRUNELLA: *(County type)* Hello, my good man – permit me to
             introduce myself. I'm Prunella Prism. Tell me, what feats
             of memory will you be demonstrating tonight?

MAN: Your orders, madam – I'm the waiter. Is there anything I
             can get you?

PRUNELLA: No, thank you – I'll have a word with this fine fellow over
             here. Hello.

BERNIE: *(Jewish)* *(Half to himself)* 071 943 0242 – 081 863 1012 –
             Oh, hello already!

PRUNELLA: Might I enquire what you're doing?

BERNIE: Memorizing all the numbers in the L to Z London
             Telephone Directory . . . *(To himself:)* 0898 6540 . . . Hot
             Sticky Thighs in . . . oh no . . . that one came out of the
             Sunday Sport, didn't it? My name's Bernie Templeman,
             by the way – but you can call me BT. So what are you
             doing here?

PRUNELLA: I recite from memory the entire works of Shakespeare . . .

BERNIE: Oi vey!

PRUNELLA: . . . backwards.

BERNIE: You what?

PRUNELLA: I recite the entire works of Shakespeare backwards – e.g.
             to wit and viz: 'Question the is that, be to not or be to.'

77

Just a soupçon, you understand – I have no wish to peak too early.

BERNIE: I quite agree. 081 788 1892 – 071 395 1092 ...

PRUNELLA: Yes, well – I mustn't interrupt your concentration any longer. 'Bleed not we do, us prick you if.' Oh! It's funny how little snippets suddenly swoop into the foreground, isn't it?

REGGIE: *(Chris as Joe Gladwin)* * 'Ow do! The name's Reggie Ramsbottom from Rotherham.

PRUNELLA: Oh, good evening. Tell me – are you eccentric?

REGGIE: No – I always dress like this.

PRUNELLA: Really. And what is that sticking out of your trousers?

REGGIE: Me ferret. That's Roderick, that is. Say hello to the nice lady, Roderick. 'E likes you. See how his little head rolls from side to side. Oh sorry – that's not Roderick.

PRUNELLA: *(Aghast)* What??!!

REGGIE: No, that's Rosemary – Roderick's lady friend.

PRUNELLA: How fascinating. And do you have an extraordinary memory?

REGGIE: Ooh, aye – lady. I remember things beginning with R.

PRUNELLA: Why?

REGGIE: I get a lot of laughs. Regular ... rhetoric ... restoration ... you see what I mean?

* *Joe Gladwin: A character actor with a broad Yorkshire accent who rolled his Rs (he did the voice-over in the Hovis commercials). Chris Emmett does a brilliant over-the-top impersonation of him.*

PRUNELLA: Truly astounding. *(Yells)* Owwww!

REGGIE: What's the matter?

PRUNELLA: Rosemary bit me!

REGGIE: No, that weren't Rosemary.

PRUNELLA: But I saw her poke out of your pocket and go straight for my hand. It must have been Roderick then.

REGGIE: Weren't Roderick neither.

PRUNELLA: *(Horrified, wiping her hand down her front)* Oh, my stars!

REGGIE: It were Rambo. He's an inquisitive little rascal. Come on, Rambo – let's get you a nice glass of scrumpy . . . *(Goes off)*

(And over in another corner Dorian, a 'precious' young man, is busy practising. He is approached by two doddery old farts, Desmond and Hermoine)

DESMOND: 'Scuse me, mush. Is this the gaff where everyone is demonstrating amazing feats of memory?

DORIAN: That's quite correct.

DESMOND: Thank gawd for that! It's all right, Hermoine. We're in the right place.

HERMOINE: *(To Dorian)* Hello! So what are you here for then?

DORIAN: To demonstrate a gift that Dame Fortune has bestowed upon me. I can recall from memory the lyric of every single song in Dorothy Squire's repertoire.

HERMOINE: Are you a friend of Dorothy then?*

*A friend of Dorothy is a phrase used in homosexual and theatrical circles in reference to a man's gay proclivities. The Dorothy referred to is Dorothy Parker who had a large number of gay acquaintances and hangers-on.

DESMOND: Funny – I was about to ask the same question.

DORIAN: We've never met, actually – Dot and I – but I heard her sing last week at the Birmingham Hippodrome. I was in Scarborough at the time. Ooh, she's a loud woman, but oh so fabulous!

DESMOND: Hermoine – start the car.

DORIAN: So where do your particular talents lie then?

DESMOND: Not in your direction, chunky – that's for sure.

DORIAN: I was referring to your feats of memory.

DESMOND: Oh, them. Yes. Well, Hermoine here and myself have memorized all the positions in the *Kama Sutra*.

DORIAN: Fancy.

HERMOINE: Yers. We're the number one authority in this country on it – aren't we, Des?

DESMOND: That we are, Hermoine. And not only do we recall all the positions, sir – we demonstrate 'em an' all.

HERMOINE: Demonstrate, yers. They cancelled a performance of the Chippendales to fit us in at the Toc-H the other night – didn't they, Des?

DESMOND: Not quite, my little lotus flower, but we are in great demand.

DORIAN: I'm all agog.

DESMOND: I thought you were. I noticed that when I first walked in.

DORIAN: But how long have you been . . . er . . . demonstrating your amazing powers?

DESMOND: I think prowess is a more apt word in our case – don't you, Hermoine?

HERMOINE: Definitely. We've been committing these . . . er . . .

DORIAN: What – acts of gross indecency?

DESMOND: We prefer to call them art, sir. No, what Hermoine was trying to say is that we've been committing these love positions to memory and demonstrating them ever since we picked up the book ten years ago.

HERMOINE: Yers – the church bazaar it was.

DESMOND: Very bizarre, if you ask me. And we try and do twenty pages a night.

HERMOINE: Twenty pages, yers. Ever since we started.

DESMOND: And it's very nackering, it is.

HERMOINE: That's right. He's been in traction at least four times.

DORIAN: Well, I'm rendered totally speechless. There's one thing I must ask you though . . . er . . . it's a rather delicate question, I'm afraid.

HERMOINE: You want us to show you number 149?

DESMOND: Hermoine, Hermoine! Put your vest back on!

HERMOINE: Oh, yes – I don't want to peak too early. What was it you wanted to know?

DORIAN: Well . . . er . . . aren't you both a little old to be engaged in such a demanding activity?

DESMOND: Old! Old! Put this down to our work, mush. I'm twenty-eight and she's twenty-seven!

SPECIAL CLINIC
by Nick R. Thomas

The scene is a clinic.

DOCTOR: Well, Tracey – we can discharge your husband from this clinic today.

TRACEY: Oh thank you, doctor. But tell me, were you able to cure him of his terrible affliction?

DOCTOR: No, I'm afraid he's still Jim Davidson.

The Huddlines office receives a large number of letters from listeners, some complimentary, some not.

We reproduce some of them here:

The News Huddlines,
BBC.

Dear News Huddlines,

    As a regular listener to your show, I have to register my disapproval of
the constant use by your writers of silly names in sketches in order to procure
a cheap laugh in an otherwise amusing show.

Yours sincerely

Brigadier Margery Genitals,
69 Gonads Avenue
Littlehampton

Ms Fiona Farquaharson-Ffitch,
55 Firkin Fairway,
Firth of Forth,
Fife.

14th February 1994

Dear Mr Hudd,

Could you please do more sketches with the letter
F in them?

Felicitations,

F. F-F

Fiona Farquaharson-Ffitch

This letter arrived in the Huddlines office
handwritten in green ink ... always an
ominous sign!

tO THE CAST of tHE NEws
hUDDLinÉs

YOu F***iNG PeRvy & bAsTard
SHiTE hAWKS !

You ALL hAve sEwer miNDS likE
a rHino's BollOcks And faceS to#
mAtch. PaRTiculaRly thAt JUNE poxY
wHitField AND CHris faRt BReath emmeTT
Not To mentiON That scumBag Turd
ROY hUDD.

Your filth shOuld Be BaNned
FRom tHe aiRwavEs for EveR
You're ALL twAts!!!

your obediENt SErvAnt

Athe reveRend AmbroSe SweETie
The VicaPAGE
LaRK meaDows
GRazing-IN-THE-wOLd
dORseT.

85

Dear Roy

My partner and I are great fans of yours and we always listen to your wonderful show on our portable 'tranny', usually on a Saturday lunchtime when we're both at work.

Our place is always jumping with laughter, the staff relentlessly exchanging quips and one-liners, and we thought why not put it to good use? So could you offer us any advice on how we might write for your show and put our senses of humour to the test?

Yours hilariously

A Croak   L. Snuffit

MESSERS. CROAK & SNUFFIT
FUNERAL DIRECTORS
SLUMBERVILLE CHAPEL OF REST
FRINTON-ON-SEA
ESSEX

Roy Hudd, Esq.,
BBC,
Broadcasting House,
London W1A 1AA   20th June 1993

Dear Mr Hudd,

I listen to your show every week in a state of
permanent despair. You ridicule race, religion,
gender, politics and royalty - yet you never
deal sympathetically with minority groups.

I am President of one such organisation and I
hope that someday I can look forward to hearing
a sensitive, yet humorous sketch on the
spanking of choirboys or disciplining of
Brownies.

Yours sincerely,

Judge Peregrine Tossing-Knightly,
President of the British Paedophile Society
(Surrey Branch)
Woking,
Surrey.

BARBARA CARTLAND

Dear Huddlines

Oh, I do wish you'd have more romance and love in your show. Perhaps a Noel Coward type pastiche with lots of references to the moon and spooning and such like. Or a little playlet about a titled lady marooned on a desert island and captured by barbaric natives before being rescued by a dashing ship-wrecked mariner.

Having said that, my favourite character in your programme is Mr. Friggins. When he opens his raincoat and hear that whoosh I nearly wet myself.

I bet hes hung like a donkey.

Romantically Yours

Barbara Cartland

Publisher's Note: on checking the authenticity of this letter, in particular, the postmark, Shoreditch, we have discovered that it was written, not by *the* Barbara Cartland, but by a Babs 'Fifi' Cartland, a stripper at The Hairy Cobblers Public House in the east end of London

SUPERBABES

by **Tony Hare**

The scene is the maternity ward of a hospital.

CHARACTERS

Doctor . . . ROY HUDD
Mrs Rutherford . . . JUNE WHITFIELD
Boy baby . . . ROY HUDD
Girl baby . . . JUNE WHITFIELD

DOCTOR: Well, Mrs Rutherford – won't be long now and you'll be making history.

MRS R: Doctor – you really think that wearing that belt with the built-in speakers and playing tapes through my tummy to my unborn babies will give them a high IQ right from the start?

DOCTOR: No question – and may I congratulate you on setting up this sketch so succinctly. So, let's have a listen through my stethoscope . . . make sure all is well. *(A slight pause)* Good gracious!

MRS R: What is it, doctor?

DOCTOR: I can hear talking! I think they're having a conversation!

Meanwhile, inside Mrs Rutherford's Womb...

BOY BABY: Come on! Hurry up, woman! Get your feet in those stirrups. Nine months in here and I'm beginning to suffer from acute claustrophobia.

GIRL BABY:	You're right– I've got terrible cramp. Here, why are you curled up like that?
BOY BABY:	I'm in the foetal position.
GIRL BABY:	What's that mean?
BOY BABY:	It means my feet'll come out first.
GIRL BABY:	I'm glad I'm upside down.
BOY BABY:	Why?
GIRL BABY:	At least when I come out the view'll be better. Are you a boy or a girl?
BOY BABY:	A boy, of course.
GIRL BABY:	Oh. *(A slight pause)* What's that funny shrivelled thing on your front?
BOY BABY:	The umbilical cord. You've got one an' all. That's what's been giving us our essential food and life blood during development.
GIRL BABY:	Oh. I've been using mine for strap-hanging when she goes out in the car. They shouldn't be allowed in a car in their state. Super-intelligent I might be, but I've already got an in-built susceptibility to travel sickness.
BOY BABY:	Cor blimey – you do go on, don't you? No mistaking you're a woman.
GIRL BABY:	Don't be sexist.
BOY BABY:	What milk do you reckon we'll get – bottled or draught?
GIRL BABY:	I'm not bothered – as long as it's not that UHT rubbish she drinks. Oh, my God! What's happening? The walls are caving in!

BOY BABY:	Don't panic – the contractions have started. Won't be long now. Bags I go first.
GIRL BABY:	*I'm* in front of you and no pushing.
BOY BABY:	At least we'll have a head start on the other sprogs. We can already speak – all we've got to do is learn to walk.
GIRL BABY:	Yes, playing tapes to us all that time seems to have paid off.
BOY BABY:	But don't forget the pact we made. We're going to behave atrociously and keep them up all night with our crying and all that yucky nappy-changing stuff.
GIRL BABY:	But why?
BOY BABY:	Well, that'll be our way getting back at them for the past fortnight.
GIRL BABY:	I still don't understand.
BOY BABY:	The last tape she's been playing us over and over again!
GIRL BABY:	Oh, that one!
BOY BABY:	Yes – that bleedin' Mr Blobby single! Go on – get pushing!

THE SOUND OF MARY CHITTY-CHITTY-OLIVER-BANG-BANG-POPPINS (A Song)

Music: 'When You're Lying Awake' – *Iolanthe*

New Lyric: RICHARD QUICK

Christmas Day: The family is slumped in front of the telly following a huge lunch. Dad (ROY HUDD) has slept through the afternoon musical film. He wakes up with a start.

DAD: When I turned on the box, unprepared for such shocks,
Julie Andrews assaulted my hearing –
It was wholly unfair, and some nuns in despair
Were suggesting she try mountaineering.
So she went on a hike, where she met Dick van Dyke,
But some kids called von Trapp all pursued 'er –
Then young Oliver sang 'Chitty Chitty Bang Bang',
And proceeded to get even cruder.
He'd met Fagin and gone, when some penguins danced on,
And I'm told it's a children's best-seller,
But a nanny, who sings, did some rather strange things
With a gentleman's full-sized umbrella.

Then I had a relapse,
As the wretched von Trapps,
  Who were riding their bikes,
  While attacking Bill Sykes,
    Started asking for more
      In a candyfloss store,
        And Miss Poppins, it's true,
         Picked a pocket or two,
          But the penguins' routine
          Had been rated obscene
          By the chorus of nuns,
          Who were brandishing guns,
         So they took to the sky
        In a car that could fly –
    And the party, I'm pleased to say, broke up.

Then the credits unrolled,
And I went hot and cold,
  For the next film on view
  Was that *Ghostbusters Two* . . .
But, thank heavens, I finally woke up.

STOP PRESS

Women who are addicted to sex have been writing to Noel Edmonds.

Well, if that doesn't cure them, nothing will.

Nick R. Thomas

93

MURDOCH AND MAXWELL

by **Peter Hickey & Tony Hare**

MC:	*(June)* Ladies and gentlemen! Direct from their triumphant engagement at the Chalfont St Giles Clinic for Haemorrhoids where they made *piles* of money . . . here they are – with a smile, a song and a standing ovation – those Happy Headliners: Murdoch and Maxwell!
BAND:	*Rousing Music Hall play-on*
MAXWELL:	*(Chris)* Well, well, well – if it isn't Mucky Murdoch.
MURDOCH:	*(Roy)* And it's the broad-beamed Bobby Maxwell.
MAXWELL:	That reminds me – Gerry Cottle wants these trousers back for his winter tour.
MURDOCH:	Is that a flying trapeze you've got in there or are you just pleased to see me?
MAXWELL:	Thank gawd I've got a safety net. So, what's been happening in the news?
MURDOCH:	Well, I read that Max Bygraves has had a love child.
MAXWELL:	Yes, it was named after his first album: BonkalongaMax.
MURDOCH:	He obviously didn't need hands then. I say, there's some amazing toys out this Christmas.
MAXWELL:	Ah, you've been to Santa's Grotto in the Ann Summers shop then?

MURDOCH: No, no – I was referring to that robot dog you can buy in America.

MAXWELL: I've seen it – it's got a lot of rust under its back legs.

MURDOCH: Yes, I get the picture.

MAXWELL: And did you read about that rent boy who pinched a rail ticket from an MP's briefcase?

MURDOCH: Well, he wanted to go on an Away Gay.

MAXWELL: But there's some bad news. The EEC wants to put a stop to duty-free fags.

MURDOCH: Oh dear – no more day trips to Boulogne for Princess Margaret.

MAXWELL: Back to the Old Holborn roll-ups for her.

MURDOCH: I had a nice surprise this morning.

MAXWELL: I prefer to be woken up by the alarm clock, but there we go.

MURDOCH: No, no – I read a heart-warming story about a new hospital that's just opened for hedgehogs.

MAXWELL: And it's a great success. They've already got a two-year waiting list for spine operations.

MURDOCH: A prickly problem.

MAXWELL: And did you read about the world's oldest mini fetching eight thousand pounds?

MURDOCH: Ah, yes – it's the one worn by Barbara Cartland on her first date.

MAXWELL: Not a pretty sight.

MURDOCH: Talking of which, I see that *Star Trek*'s Captain Kirk has been ditched by his wife.

MAXWELL: Yes, and there's a bitter fight going on as to who gets custody of the wig.

MURDOCH: Here, how about that evil pong that floated across the North of England from Germany?

MAXWELL: Probably James Last on another one of his tours.

MURDOCH: And did you read about that geezer who's got a giant daffodil three foot high?

MAXWELL: That's amazing. Must have been attracted by the light.

MURDOCH: Quite true – mine as well.

MAXWELL: Your what?

MURDOCH: My daffodil – what's yours called?

MAXWELL: None of your business – kindly leave the flower bed. But pass me the Gro-bag before you go.

MURDOCH: And how about that Reverend who's qualified as a chiropodist?

MAXWELL: That's right. But he does get mixed up. At last Sunday's communion he dished out Odour Eaters and Radox.

MURDOCH: I thought those wafers were a bit chewy.

MAXWELL: But you see some funny things, don't you?

MURDOCH: Not since the mirror fell off the ceiling.

MAXWELL: No, listen – I couldn't believe that story I read about a geezer who used a photo booth to take pictures of his groin injuries.

MURDOCH: Well, it does say: 'Wait For The Flash'. And what about that crazy motorist who changed a wheel in the fast lane?

MAXWELL: Ridiculous. You'd think he'd have slowed down while doing it, wouldn't you?

MURDOCH: Yes – you should have seen the skid marks.

MAXWELL: There's no answer to that. And, moving hastily on, I see they've introduced speed traps for boats on the Norfolk Broads.

MURDOCH: Yes, but the scheme's not a success.

MAXWELL: Oh, why is that?

MURDOCH: Well, the police have sunk four panda-cars trying to chase them.

MAXWELL: And now their truncheons have got rising damp.

MURDOCH: They always shrink in the water, you know.

MAXWELL: Here's one that'll put you off your dinner.

MURDOCH: Don't tell me Andrew Lloyd Webber's in the news again.

MAXWELL: He is, but that's not the story. A bloke has become a champion after eating a pound of eels in thirty-two seconds.

MURDOCH: That's right – he trained for it by chewing Wrigleys.

MAXWELL: A little play on words there, folks.

MURDOCH: Did you read about that candidate for the Monster Raving Loony Party who's going to tattoo their policies on his chest?

MAXWELL: Yes – and you should see where he's putting his election address.

MURDOCH: But there won't be any room for the post code.

MAXWELL: Well, most of the time. Now here's a funny thing . . .

MURDOCH: Well, put it away.

MAXWELL: No, listen! A Japanese firm is making clothes out of pineapples.

MURDOCH: Doesn't half make for chunky Y-fronts.

MAXWELL: Boasting again!

MURDOCH: Which reminds me, Tom Jones has returned to Britain.

MAXWELL: But he won't be working here for a while as he's had to put his trousers into quarantine.

MURDOCH: I see there's a new survey out that says parents are too thick to help with their kids' homework.

MAXWELL: Absolutely disgraceful. I mean, you know all about algebra, don't you?

MURDOCH: Never been there. I prefer Benidorm myself.

MAXWELL: Here, did you read about that star from *EastEnders* who did a strip at a gay club for charity?

MURDOCH: I wish I'd seen it.

MAXWELL: You should have – he raised quite a bit!

BOTH: Aye, aye – that's yer lot!

BAND: *Rousing music-hall play-off*

EAT YER HEART OUT, LAWRENCE OF ARABIA

by Malcolm Williamson

CHARACTERS

Prince Charles . . . CHRIS EMMETT

Kalahari Tribesman . . . ROY HUDD

Kalahari Tribeswoman . . . JUNE WHITFIELD

Prince Charles was so worried about the chaos of modern life, he went off into the depths of the Kalahari Desert to meet the Kalahari Bushmen, the only remaining tribe in the world untouched by civilization. He could have achieved the same ends by spending an afternoon at Stamford Bridge, but there you go. The Huddlines *caught up with His Vegetarianness in the remotest part of the African Bush to see how his soul-searching got on.*

SOUND FX: *Sounds of the African Bush and clip-clop of camel's hooves*

CHARLES: *(Singing)* Well, I'm the King of the Swingers, a jungle VIP . . .

SOUND FX: *Camel roar*

CHARLES: Oh, dear – one's jolly old camel is a bit cream-crackered, I fear. OK, Dobbin . . . down.

SOUND FX: *Camel grunting*

CHARLES: Ooh, crikey – that's better! Now I know why they call them the ship of the desert – you have to make sure you don't sit on the funnel. Now I wonder where the Bushmen are . . .

(Tribal noises, African chanting and grunts – tribesman and tribeswoman approach, singing)

'Daylight come and I wanna go home . . .'

TRIBESMAN: Hello, matey – we are from the lost tribe of the Kalahari.

CHARLES: Gosh. Where do you live?

TRIBESMAN: I don't know – we're lost. Let me introduce myself. My sacred name is The One On Whom The Dandruff Never Settles.

TRIBESWOMAN: And my sacred name is She for Whom Alone the Sap Rises.

TRIBESMAN: Do you have a sacred name?

CHARLES: Yes – He Who Resembles a Walking Toby Jug. Now listen. I've come to discover the secrets of your way of life.

TRIBESMAN: Then we tell you in song and dance. Ready? And one, two!

(Tribal drums, tribesman and woman sing)

TRIBESWOMAN: We are the Kalahari . . .
TRIBESMAN: And we live here in the Bush,
TRIBESWOMAN: If you break our laws . . .
TRIBESMAN: Then we'll smack you in the mush.

CHARLES: Jolly impressive. What else do you do at your ceremonies?

TRIBESMAN: We commune with the spirit of the desert by wailing.

CHARLES: Cor, I'd be good at that.

TRIBESWOMAN: Why?

CHARLES: Well, I am the Prince of Wales. That's what we in the West call a joke.

TRIBESMAN: It's what we in the East call a load of boll . . .

TRIBESWOMAN: *(Interrupting)* Well, Mr Prince, perhaps you're hungry. We can offer you our local delicacy: ostrich.

CHARLES: Ostrich? Do you catch the birds yourselves?

TRIBESMAN: Oh, no – we just nip down to the Kalahari Fried Ostrich. Very handy. They come with their heads stuck in a cardboard bucket.

CHARLES: Staying on the physical plane for just a moment, how do you Bush folk go about producing the patter of tiny feet?

TRIBESMAN: Oh, blimey. Well, there's the mummy and the daddy . . .

CHARLES: No, no. I mean, where do you do it?

TRIBESMAN Oh, I see. Well, once a year, all the Bushmen in the tribe go off into the scrub with their mates . . .

TRIBESWOMAN: Known as Scrubbers.

CHARLES: Then what happens?

TRIBESMAN: I'm not really sure, but there's an awful lot of beating about the bush.

TRIBESWOMAN: So, Mr Prince – have you learned much from our spiritual way of life?

CHARLES: Not half. There's a tremendous feeling of peace and serenity here. The fact that I'm standing where no white man has stood before makes me tingle right down to my toes.

TRIBESMAN: I'm not surprised, matey. You may be standing where no white man has been, but unfortunately, you're standing right where the camel has!

SOUND FX: *Squelch*

CHARLES: Oh, crikey!

STOP PRESS

A man tried to smuggle four parrots hidden inside his trousers.

When the Customs Officer asked, "Anything to declare?" The parrots shouted, "Not a lot!"

Gerry Goddin

STOP PRESS

New satellite pictures of Venus prove it to be a living hell.

So they've renamed it Bromley.

Oleh Stepaniuk

A *Huddlines* script goes through quite a transition from the original draft lovingly honed by the writer.

The producer might make minor alterations, but it is during the read-through on a Thursday morning when the most changes take place, the cast gagging it up here and there, making subtle adjustments to the lines.

Overleaf is an example of just one page, complete with the cast's comments . . .

1. JUNE: I am bidding you welcome to my school. Allow me
                to be introducing one of my colleagues, Boris
                Tchaikowski.

2. ROY: (RUSSIAN) Watcha cocker! I think that is being
                the typical greeting in your country, da?

3. CHRIS: Close. Boris Tchaikowski? You're no relation to
                the great composer, are you?

4. ROY: Certainly not! I'm straight. Though I must be
                confessing to a slight fondness for your Dorothy
                Squires.

5. JUNE: And I am Yvonne Korsakov.

6. CHRIS: Pleased to meet you. Are you the principal of
                this school?

7. JUNE: No - the dinner lady. I was just the menu for the
                day to Mr Tchaikowski showing.

8. ROY: Today Yvonne is giving us Potato Peel soup for
                starters, followed by Fricasee of Beetroot in a
                Vodka Sauce and cabbage and custard for pudding.

9. JUNE: Yum-yum-nya.

10. CHRIS: And are you a good cook?

WREN THE BOAT COMES IN
by Tony Hare

CHARACTERS

Admiral . . . CHRIS EMMETT

Chief Petty Officer . . . ROY HUDD

Able Seaman . . . JUNE WHITFIELD

Meanwhile, in an office at the Admiralty . . .

ADMIRAL:	Further to your letter of the 18th inst, Able Seaman Golightly was found clinging to a buoy in the English Channel, but we shall provide the best defence Her Majesty's Navy can muster. I remain, yours sincerely, Rear-Admiral Sir Francis Limpet.
SOUND FX:	*Knock on door*
ADMIRAL:	Yes, what is it?
CPO:	*(Off)* Prisoner and escort to see you, sah.
ADMIRAL:	Enter.
SOUND FX:	*Door open – one set of quick-marching footsteps*
CPO:	Left, right, left, right, left, right – Halt!
SOUND FX:	*Footsteps halt*

CPO:	Thumbs in line with the seams of your Y-fronts!
ADMIRAL:	And you are?
CPO:	Chief Petty Officer Rollocks, sah. Currently serving on the frigate *Sodit*.
ADMIRAL:	The frigate *Sodit*?
CPO:	That's what the Lady Mayoress named it at the launch when the champagne bottle wouldn't break.
ADMIRAL:	I see. And what is the name of your prisoner?
CPO:	The prisoner's name is listed in the ship's log as Able Seaman Horatio Thug, sah.
ADMIRAL:	And a fine figure of a man he is too.
ABLE SEAMAN:	*(Deep voice)* Thank you, sir. You're very kind.
CPO:	Don't let appearances fool you, sah. It is but a devious disguise. I have reason to believe that Able Seaman Horatio Thug is in fact . . . a woman!
ADMIRAL:	*(Aghast)* What?! You mean one of those chaps with squeaky voices and water wings at the front?
CPO:	The very same, sah.
ADMIRAL:	Disgraceful!
ABLE SEAMAN:	*(Deep voice)* It's not true, sir. I'm definitely a geezer.
CPO:	Be quiet! You can have your say in a minute.
ADMIRAL:	How long has Able Seaman Thug served in her Majesty's Navy, CPO?
CPO:	Six days. I first became suspicious whilst carrying out the entrance examination in my other capacity as Medical Orderly.

ADMIRAL:	Medical Orderly?
CPO:	Yes, sah. Naval cuts you know. I'm also ship's cook, chief stoker and I do a spot of moonlighting as a singing telegram.
ADMIRAL:	I'll remember that for our next Admiralty dinner. *(Sotto)* You don't happen to have a scoutmaster's uniform, do you?
CPO:	I'll see what I can lay my hands on, sah.
ADMIRAL:	So what happened at the medical?
CPO:	When asked to strip off, Able Seaman Thug showed great reluctance, but was eventually persuaded. I then asked the prisoner to account for the strange formation of his . . . er . . . chest – if you'll pardon the expression. I received the reply that it was the unfortunate result of a childhood malady called Dropped Mumps.
ABLE SEAMAN:	*(Deep voice)* It's perfectly true. I got 'em as a boy.
CPO:	I won't tell you again, sailor.
ABLE SEAMAN:	*(Deep voice – muttering)* Hardly worth my being in this sketch!
ADMIRAL:	Carry on, Rollocks.
CPO:	But then, upon closer medical examination my suspicions were confirmed. When asking the prisoner to cough, something which shouldn't have, came off in my hand.
ADMIRAL:	What?!
CPO:	The prisoner had stuck it on to authenticate the disguise.
ADMIRAL:	You don't mean . . .
CPO:	I do. A false beard.

ADMIRAL: That's a relief.

CPO: Ginger.

ADMIRAL: Less of the familiarity, Petty Officer. Only my closest friends call me that.

CPO: No, no, sah. The beard was ginger.

ADMIRAL: Ah. Strike my last remark from the record then.

CPO: It was then, sah – I was convinced we had become the victims of a major deception.

ADMIRAL: Major Deception? He's one of those army wallahs, isn't he?

CPO: Only on his mother's side, sah.

ADMIRAL: Well, young feller-me-lass – what have you got to say for yourself?

ABLE SEAMAN: *(Female voice)* All right sir – I've been rumbled. I admit it – I *am* a woman. But when I read last week that the Wrens were being disbanded I was desperate. All my life I've wanted to swing a hammock, handle a sextant and enjoy a hornpipe. This subterfuge seemed the only way of joining up.

CPO: You stupid bint. You didn't need to go to all that trouble. The Navy has accepted women for years now.

ADMIRAL: It has? Then why wasn't I informed?

CPO: It was in all the papers.

ADMIRAL: Thank God for that – now I can get rid of this damned false beard and corset.

                SOUND FX: *Velcro rip – two boings*

ADMIRAL: *(Thunderthighs*)* Ah, that's better!

CPO: Good heavens! Mother!

*Thunderthighs is a character Chris Emmett plays, reminiscent of Dame Edith Evans.

STOP PRESS

Arnold Schwarzenegger is to become pregnant in a forthcoming film.

His new catchphrase will be: "Ooh, me back!"

Gerry Goddin

MAGGOT-VENDING MACHINE

by Nick R. Thomas

1ST MAN: *(Whistling)* 'Morning.

2ND MAN: 'Morning. My! That's an impressive rod you've got there. I bet you're proud of that!

1ST MAN: Yes, I am. In fact, I'm just off fishing with it right now. But I thought I'd stop on the way and try out this new maggot-vending machine. You just put your coins in here, like this, press this button, and yes, here we are – out come the maggots to use as bait. I say – are you feeling OK? You've gone very pale.

2ND MAN: So would you if you'd just put coins in a vending machine and drunk what you thought was a lumpy cup of noodle soup!

(He throws up)

HAIRY FRIGGINS

by Tony Hare

DOCTOR: Next patient, please.

SOUND FX: *Door opening*

FRIGGINS: 'Mornin', doctor!

DOCTOR: Mr Friggins! What seems to be the trouble?

FRIGGINS: Well, you know that stuff scientists have been working on which grows hair in a test tube?

DOCTOR: Yes – it looks like at long last there's a medical breakthrough in restoring hair loss.

FRIGGINS: I can tell you, it works. I got hold of some.

DOCTOR: I was afraid you might have.

FRIGGINS: Oh, yes. I was standing on the draining board yesterday having a strip–wash like you do – and I put some of that stuff on my head, but as I sat down in the sink to wash me feet I knocked the bottle over and it landed in me lap.

DOCTOR: *(Anticipating the worst)* Ye-e-s.

FRIGGINS: Well, I woke up this morning and this had happened.

SOUND FX: *Whoosh*

DOCTOR: Good lord! Er, does it hurt?

FRIGGINS: Only when I lean forward.

DOCTOR:	I'm not surprised. Do you mind if I have another look?
FRIGGINS:	My pleasure, Doctor.
DOCTOR:	I'm sure it is. I can't say the same for me.
SOUND FX:	*Whoosh*
DOCTOR:	My, my. Well, there's only one thing for it. Where's the phone?
SOUND FX:	*Dialling of phone*
FRIGGINS:	Who are you ringing? Another doctor for a second opinion?
DOCTOR:	No – David Attenborough.
FRIGGINS:	David Attenborough? What on earth for?
DOCTOR:	Well, it's the first time I've seen a couple of hedgehogs and a hairy caterpillar nesting in the same place!

STOP PRESS

A new medical study has revealed the dangers of bell-ringing.

The chief one is getting your ding-dong caught merrily on high.

Tony Wheatley

112

MAJOR'S ENORMOUS ELECTION

by **Mike Coleman**

The Scene: Inside Number 10.

CHARACTERS

John Major . . . ROY HUDD

Norma Major . . . JUNE WHITFIELD

JOHN: *(To himself)* What's it to be, a November election or wait till next year? This is my big chance to show how decisive I can be . . . Eeny-meeny-miny-mo.

(The door opens, and Norma enters, singing)

NORMA: John . . .

JOHN: Yes, my little Nessun Norma?

NORMA: Is Mr Kissikins coming to bed, John? Mrs Snoggypuss is getting cold.

JOHN: *(Preoccupied)* Mmmm, Baker says we should have it now.

NORMA: What's it got to do with Baker when we have it?

JOHN: I think I'd prefer to wait until May.

NORMA: Wait until May? If you think I'm . . .

113

JOHN:	For the election, my little angel.
NORMA:	Oh, I see. Well, if Baker suggests having it now, there's your answer. When was he ever right?
JOHN:	You mustn't talk about Mr Baker like that, Norma – he's a highly respected member of the Government.
NORMA:	No, he's not – he's a walking disaster: The Poll Tax, the Education Act and now Law and Order. With a track record like that, he should be running British Rail.
JOHN:	I know, Norma - but he could be right this time. My problem is I can't really believe we're so high in the polls.
NORMA:	It's you, John – it's your charisma.
JOHN:	*(Dully)* Oh, yes.
NORMA:	People trust you to put things right.
JOHN:	*(Tearful)* Oh, Norma . . . everyone's being so . . . you know . . .
NORMA:	Gullible?
JOHN:	'Nice', I was going to say.
NORMA:	Exactly. So come to bed with Mrs Snoggypuss and leave all this worrying to the Prime Minister.
JOHN:	Oh, all right. . . *(He thinks)* Hang on . . .
NORMA:	What now?
JOHN:	I *am* the Prime Minister.
NORMA:	Don't be silly, John.
JOHN:	But I am.

NORMA:	Rubbish! I'd have noticed. Anyway, I've seen him on the telly: he's a rather nondescript boring little man with . . . Ooo-er . . . it *is* you, isn't it?
JOHN:	Of course it's me. That's why I've been working so hard. Do you know I was up until nearly nine o'clock last night?
NORMA:	Oh, thank heavens for that, John – I thought you must be having an . . . with another . . . well, you know what a SEX bomb you are.
JOHN:	Silly Norma! I'd never miss our nightly games.
NORMA:	*(Sexily)* Mmmmmmm. *(She snuggles up to him)*
JOHN:	You know how I can't do without my Scrabble.
NORMA:	Just so long as you're not double-scoring with anyone else, that's all. *(Seductive)* Oh, John – why don't you put a record on right now, my heart throb?
JOHN:	No, Norma – what about my duty as a Statesman? Norma, stop doing that . . . Norma . . . Oh, I say . . . um . . . which record would you like?
NORMA:	You decide.
JOHN:	Right. *(A slight pause)* Eeny-meeny-miny-mo . . .
NORMA:	*(Sighs)* Just put anything on, Kissikins.

(John puts a record on the gramophone. We hear locomotive engines)

NORMA:	What's that?
JOHN:	'Great steam locomotives of the LMS, 1945-53' – it's my favourite . . .
NORMA:	Tell you what, let's forget the soft music . . .

(The record is scratched off)

JOHN:	Careful with my stylus, Norma!
NORMA:	Ooh, John – let me run my fingers through your hair. *(Matter of fact)* Urrgh, you need an oil change. *(Seductive again)* Now, take off your glasses.
JOHN:	Like this?
NORMA:	Yes, yes . . . My God, John – you're . . .
JOHN:	Yes?
NORMA:	*(Disappointed)* Exactly the same. Never mind, leave them off and . . . kiss me . . .
JOHN:	Right. *(A slight pause)* Um . . . where are you, Norma?
NORMA:	What?
JOHN:	Only I can't see you without my . . .
NORMA:	Oh, John! I'm a woman with a woman's needs. You don't understand a woman's . . . appetites . . .
JOHN:	Of course I do, my angel! *(A slight pause)* I'll get the Chocolate Hobnobs.
NORMA:	Oh John, you mad crazy fool! Quick, while the mood's on me . . .
JOHN:	*(Assertive)* No. I mustn't. Duty awaits. I must sort out when to have the next election.
NORMA:	But why . . .? Why now?
JOHN:	Isn't it obvious?
NORMA:	No.

JOHN: To give myself as long as possible to decide.

NORMA: The date of the election?

JOHN: No, no . . .

NORMA: What then?

JOHN: Who I'm going to vote for.

STOP PRESS

A new 85 mile an hour terror ride is coming to Blackpool

It's called a drive with the Marquis of Blandford.

Oleh Stepaniuk

OVER THE TOPOL

a short story by **Peter Hickey**

CHARACTERS

Menahem Golan, movie mogul . . . ROY HUDD

Yoram Globus, movie mogul . . . CHRIS EMMETT

Meryl Strap, an actress . . . JUNE WHITFIELD

The film world was shattered when it was announced that Pinewood Studios, for many decades the home of J. Arthur Rank – that well known movie company and rhyming slang – was closing down. In future, producers would have to find alternative accommodation – but where would they go . . .?

Menahem Golan was seated behind a makeshift desk in his heavily Jewish trailer which he called his Winnebagel, smoking a large cigar and reading the script of *Deathwish 24*, when the door opened and his partner, Yoram Globus, burst in. He was somewhat agitated, chicken soup splashed over the paper napkin still tucked in his collar.

'Quick, Menahem!' he gesticulated. 'She's here! Our new star! Meryl Strap!'

Menahem looked up from his manuscript, calmly. 'Already?' he said.

'Actually, Menahem,' replied Yoram. 'She's late.'

'I know,' said Golan with a shrug, 'I just always say "already".'

A car drew up outside. The two men stepped into the sunlight to greet their new arrival. Meryl Strap was already out of the chauffeur-driven Lada.

'Ah, Meryl! Welcome to Firewood Studios – home of *Superman 5*,' gushed Menahem.

When Meryl spoke it was with an Afro-Geordie-Canadian accent: 'How long will we be shooting?'

'Until the Scouts want their hut back,' replied Yoram. His partner took her by the arm.

'Let us show you around,' he said. And he opened the creaky wooden door of the Scout Hut to allow her admittance. He pointed towards the end of the hut. 'This is Stage 2 where we've built the massive set of the Planet Teflon . . .'

'The asteroid with the non-stick surface,' added Yoram.

Miss Strap was not impressed. 'Very impressive,' she said. 'What was this area used for before?'

Menahem answered her question. 'This is where the Boy Scouts did their whittling.'

'Oh yes,' agreed Yoram. 'Very handy with the penknives, they are. Five of them have already got their Grade One Rabbi's Badge.'

Meryl studied the set. 'It says in my script I have to run down miles and miles of corridors in the Daily Planet building. Where do I do that?'

'It's the passage between the Brownies' and Cubs' changing rooms,' Menahem told her.

'But that's only about twelve feet.'

'OK, already. We just keep changing the wallpaper.'

For some reason, Meryl didn't seem convinced. She approached a closed door and asked what was on the other side of it. Yoram obligingly opened it to satisfy her curiosity. There was a huge explosion and he slammed it shut quickly.

Meryl exclaimed: 'My God! What was that?'

'That was the Gents,' said Globus. 'Only we're using it for Special Effects,' he added.

'But there was a man in there,' said Meryl.

Menahem chipped in: 'He's our pyrotechnics expert, Abie Astra. He was trying out a few flashes.'

'It was the explosions I was worried about,' Meryl retorted.

'It's the gefilte fishfingers that do it,' said Yoram.

Meryl thought for a moment. 'That reminds me,' she said, 'Do you have a canteen here?'

'Do we have a canteen? Do we have a canteen?' scoffed Golan, an incredulous tone in his voice. Then he said, 'Well, to be truthful – it's a camp fire at the back.'

'But it *is* kosher,' Globus assured her.

'*And* wholesale,' added Golan.

Meryl Strap studied the two men, as if sizing them up. 'There are a few things in the script I don't understand,' she said. 'For instance, why is Clark Kent now called Clark Goldstein?'

'Copyright problems,' said Menahem, puffing on his cigar.

'And what happened to the deadly Kryptonite?' asked Meryl.

Golan replied, 'Same reason – but we've overcome that. Now Superman is robbed of his superpowers by a British Rail pork pie.'

Miss Strap nodded her head. 'I know the feeling. And what about the flying sequences?'

'All done with models,' Menahem told her. He turned to his partner. 'Yoram, show her your miniatures.'

'I can't,' replied the other movie mogul. 'They're in the wife's name.'

Still the leading actress wasn't satisfied. 'What about the final confrontation between good and evil?' she asked.

'The VAT man's not coming till next week,' was Golan's answer to that question.

'No, no,' said Meryl. 'I mean Lex Lucre, as you've now called him. It says in the script that there's a really spectacular duel to the death between him and Superman in the Ice Kingdom.'

'That's right, Meryl, my little yenta – a duel to the death in the Ice Kingdom,' reiterated Menahem.

'And where are you going to shoot it?'

'In a deep freeze at Bejams.'

Meryl threw her script down in disgust and said, 'Well, I'm sorry, but this is ridiculous. You can't possibly film the kind of production this is supposed to be in these tacky surroundings.'

'Why not?' Menahem grunted, 'We do all right with the Stallone films.'

His partner chipped in. 'Anyway, already – where could we find the huge open space we need that's always empty?'

Meryl smiled at him. 'But I know just the place,' she said.

Both men, feeling a tagline coming on, spoke together: 'You do? My life! Where?'

Meryl delivered her final salvo: 'Where else? Fulham Football Ground!'

STOP PRESS

An ink factory exploded in Sydney, Australia, causing extensive damage.

Now neighbours are saying it's a blot on the landscape.

Gerry Goddin

STOP PRESS

Prince Charles is planning to build 900 houses in The Duchy of Cornwall.

Well—he wants to make sure Diana never finds him.

Tony Farrer

STOP PRESS

A police cadet had his bottom bitten by five Constables.

Honestly—the Things you have to do to get into the Masons.

Oleh Stepaniuk

122

THE HUDDLINES ANNUAL ON

LAW AND ORDER

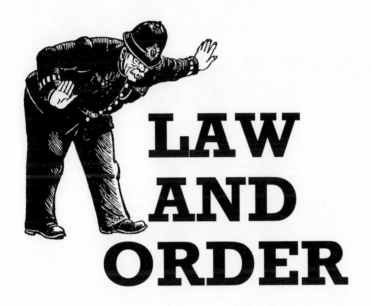

I RABBIT'S STEW IN THE NAME OF THE LAWN

by Stuart Silver

CHARACTERS

Police Sergeant . . . ROY HUDD

WPC . . . JUNE WHITFIELD

Police Constable . . . CHRIS EMMETT

*One Easter, not so long ago, a man held up a bank while dressed as a rabbit –
apparently he told the manager, to hand over the cabbage. Unconfirmed reports
claim that the police put him in a cell with another rabbit impersonator and
when they looked in an hour later they had five thousand suspects. So the
Huddlines hared round to Scotland Yard to watch the newly formed Bunny
Burglar Force in action.*

SOUND FX:	*Intercom Buzzer*
SERGEANT:	Hello? Fluffy Squad here. Sergeant Bright Eyes speaking.
WPC:	*(Distort*)* Sir. This is WPC Watership Down. Your undercover partner's just arrived.
SERGEANT:	Ah, he probably needs fresh straw for the squad car. Send him in.

** Distort – Electronic doctoring of the human voice to make it sound like it's on
the other end of a telephone.*

SOUND FX:	*Door opening – Followed by a series of 'Boings'*
SERGEANT:	Hello, Hutch.
CONSTABLE:	*(Makes toothy noises like rabbits do)* Hello, Boss. Can you take me off this undercover work? Last night I got mugged by Basil Brush.
SERGEANT:	Really?
CONSTABLE:	Yes – I'll be bug . . . bug . . . bug . . . Bugs Bunnied if I'm going out there again. Look, I don't feel well – I want to go home.
SERGEANT:	Don't start that lark again – pretending you're ill.
CONSTABLE:	Pretending, sir?
SERGEANT:	Yeah – last week you told me you had myxomatosis. Now get hopping. On second thoughts stay here – I want you to meet someone.
SOUND FX:	*Intercom buzzer*
SERGEANT:	WPC Watership Down? In here.
WPC:	*(Distort)* Coming, sir.
SOUND FX:	*Screeching tyres, fast car halts. Machine gun.*
SERGEANT:	Who the hell are you meant to be?
WPC:	Bunny and Clyde.
SERGEANT:	Look you two – we're supposed to be dealing with this outbreak of rabbit robbers – they're vicious. Some of 'em behave like animals.
CONSTABLE:	Really, sir?
SERGEANT:	Yes, Hutch. This one 'ere, this rabbit's wanted for robbery

with a sawn-off carrot. Here's his description.

CONSTABLE: *(Reading)* Small, white . . . with whiskers?

WPC: Sir, we're holding a suspect who matches this description!

SERGEANT: Really? Who is it?

WPC: David Kossoff.

CONSTABLE: Ah yes – there's a warren out for his arrest.

SERGEANT: Enough of these terrible Bugs Bunny type jokes! Have you caught that gang of desperate rabbits yet?

WPC: Desperate rabbits? Oh dear . . . there must've been a typing error, sir.

SERGEANT: Why – who have you got in there?

SOUND FX: *Door opening*

CROWD: *(Heavily Jewish)* Oy, oy, oy! Gevalt! My life! Matzos! Already! Sir Lew Grade! etc.

SOUND FX: *Door shuts*

SERGEANT: I said rabbits, not rabbis!

SOUND FX: *Phone rings. receiver is picked up*

SERGEANT: Hello? . . . Yes . . . Thank you.

SOUND FX: *Phone receiver replaced on cradle*

SERGEANT: We've cracked it, lads! That was my informant ringing from the pet shop.

WPC: *(A gasp)* What did he say?

SERGEANT: *(Imitating a parrot)* Pieces of eight, pieces of eight! *(Own voice)* But he also said the gang bungled a robbery of the pet shop.

CONSTABLE: What went wrong?

SERGEANT: Well, somebody shouted: 'Hand over the doe' and everyone jumped over the counter. Now the gang's hiding out in a bungalow. So the question is, how do we know which bungalow the rabbits are in?

CONSTABLE: Simple sir. It'll be the one with chicken wire grille and a bottle of water sticking out the window.

SERGEANT: Well done, lad. You'll get extra lettuce for this. Now then – any suggestions as to how we find this bungalow?

CONSTABLE: Yes, sir. We follow the trail of those little brown things.

SERGEANT: Maltesers?

WPC: Ho yes, sir. Rabbits have a very sweet tooth.

CONSTABLE: Thank goodness for that.

SERGEANT: Come on, men – case solved.

CONSTABLE: Just a minute, sir. When we get to the house, how do we actually flush the rabbit robbers out?

SERGEANT: Ah – simple, lad. WPC, break out the ferret costumes!

A QUICKIE

SUITABLE PUNISHMENT

by **Gerry Goddin**

Down at the local nick an interrogation is in progress.

CHARACTERS

Policeman . . . ROY HUDD

Policewoman . . . JUNE WHITFIELD

Suspect . . . CHRIS EMMETT

POLICEMAN: Do you deny that you stole anything from that supermarket, Basher?

SUSPECT: 'Course I do, copper.

WPC: Then how do you account for this bag of sausages we found stuffed down your trousers?

POLICEMAN: And these pork chops . . .

WPC: And this packet of bacon . . .

SUSPECT: Beats me.

POLICEMAN: Right, Basher – Policewoman Flighty and I have had enough lip from you. You're going to get the punishment you deserve.

WPC: Absolutely. You've got it coming to you.

SUSPECT: You don't mean . . . ?

POLICEMAN: Yes, sunbeam – you're in for a mixed grilling.

BUCK HOUSE, ACID HOUSE

by **Ged Parsons**

CHARACTERS

Roger Thrust, (The Brummie Reporter) . . . CHRIS EMMETT

Police Sergeant . . . ROY HUDD

WPC . . . JUNE WHITFIELD

ROGER:	Hello! This is Roger Thrust, your roving investigative reporter with another red-hot exposé. I'm standing outside Buckingham Palace, the scene of an outrage that has left the public shocked and speechless . . . I mean, *three pounds fifty* for a hot-dog and a lukewarm Fanta?! It's scandalous – it really is. Not only that, but this week saw rumours of alleged drug-dealing within the Palace grounds. I'm now joined by the special police squad responsible for the investigation. Hello.
SERGEANT:	Hello.
WPC:	Hello.
ROGER:	You are Sergeant Tom Pepper?
SERGEANT:	Correct.
ROGER:	CID?
SERGEANT:	No – TOM. Otherwise I'd be Sid, wouldn't I, sir? And this bright young lady is WPC Wandsworth – famous for her little grey cells.

ROGER:	I see. And those are the drugs you confiscated?
SERGEANT:	Yes, indeed. *(Sniffs)* 100% pure. Believe me, sir – this stuff is evil. It affects your memory, destroys your moral fibre, and affects your memory.
ROGER:	And am I right in thinking you two led the dramatic dawn swoop on the Palace?
SERGEANT:	Giraffe.
WPC:	Yes, yes, Roger – that is correct. It *was* planned as a dramatic *midnight* swoop, but the station tandem got a puncture and we arrived six hours late.
ROGER:	Six hours? To mend a puncture?
SERGEANT:	Well it was dark, sir – and I *had* spent five hours trying to pump up the tyre with my truncheon – an easy mistake to make.
ROGER:	So how were your suspicions first raised?
WPC:	It all started when the sergeant here had an unexpected tip-off.
ROGER:	Oh, bad luck.
SERGEANT:	But after a week's sick leave I was back on the case. We had received documentary proof that there was some dope at the Palace.
ROGER:	Ah – a hidden video camera?
SERGEANT:	No – Princess Diana's CSE results. It was then we decided on a get-tough policy – but, sadly, the 'Keep Off The Grass' signs didn't work. So, we went undercover.
ROGER:	How exciting! What happened?
SERGEANT:	To blend into the Royal surroundings, WPC Wandsworth

	and I donned red tight-fitting tunics, heavy boots and large silly hats.
ROGER:	And you both got in disguised as Guardsmen?
WPC:	No, we both got in disguised as Fergie.
SERGEANT:	Dirty work, sir – but someone's got to do it. *(Sniffs)* This stuff is evil, sir, *evil*! Deck-chair.
WPC:	Anyway, our plan was working. Almost immediately, we encountered . . . the fence.
ROGER:	Ah – police slang for the criminal go-between, or middle-man?
SERGEANT:	No – police slang for twenty-five foot of cast-iron railings.
ROGER:	Oh, silly me . . . sorry.
SERGEANT:	A common mistake for the layman, sir – it's easily done.
ROGER:	And how did you deal with this fence?
SERGEANT:	We dug it up and held it for forty-eight hours, but it told us nothing. We were getting nowhere.
ROGER:	Yes, I know the feeling. But how did you find the drugs?
SERGEANT:	All thanks to our secret weapon.
WPC:	Our faithful pedigree sniffer corgi . . . Alex Hurricane Frank Bough of Blandford.
CORGI:	*(Excited yelps)*
SERGEANT:	Down, boy! Down! PC Percy Edwards is a little swine, he really is. Down, I say!
ROGER:	Down? You'll be lucky. That dog looks as high as a kite. So, this case is solved then.

SERGEANT: Absolutely – and we've the evidence right here. *(Sniff)* Cor, it *is* evil stuff, sir. *(He is now well stoned and starts singing:)* I'm out of my head in Buckingham Palace . . .

ROGER: So, as a result of your success, you've both been promoted.

WPC: Yes – I'm off to Special Branch . . .

ROGER: And what about you, Sergeant?

SERGEANT: Where else, man? Me and the corgi are joining the Flying Squad! Far out! Wheeeeee!

THE IMAGE
by Tony Farrer

A police sergeant and constable are in conference at the local nick.

SERGEANT: *(Chris)* Constable – I see from your report that you apprehended a motorist doing seventy miles an hour in a built-up area and yet you didn't charge him.

CONSTABLE: *(Roy)* That's right, Sarge.

SERGEANT: Well done, Constable. Was that because of our new softly-softly approach to motorists to improve the policeman's image?

CONSTABLE: No, Sarge. It was because of the Chief Inspector's uniform he was wearing.

Overheard from members of the studio audience as they leave after a recording of *The News Huddlines*:

'Laugh? I filled up my incontinent pants'

'I was very disappointed Vince Hill didn't come on. Chris Emmett's voice isn't as good as Vince's

'Pliss? I am don't can't be understanding da Eengleesh. It seems to are being funny, but we are thinking we had been coming to *Noel's House Party*'

'You got a fag? I only come in out of the cold'

'You thieving bastard! You scoffed all the rich tea fingers!'

'Roy Hudd? Bloody fool. It's time he retired'

'They do them in a smaller size in Dorothy Perkins'

'Christ! I need a drink'

'You wouldn't think June Whitfield needed the work, would you?'

'F***ing commissionaires! They're worse than the Gestapo'

'I must come again next week. I didn't believe it this time'

'You've got to be a poof to do what they do'

'Course, they're *all* poofs at the BBC'

'Roy Hudd doesn't look like a poof, does he?'

'I've heard at least one of the writers is'

'That bloke behind me never stopped laughing – I've got biscuit crumbs all down the back of my neck!'

'Chris Emmett? A sex change? Never!'

'If you don't behave yourself, young lady – I'll make you listen to the show tonight!'

1st Lady: 'That Roy Hudd should never wear those Lycra shorts at his age. He hasn't got the legs for it'

2nd Lady: 'I wasn't looking at his legs'

'It's much funnier than Weekending, isn't it?'

WRINKLIES IN LOVE

a short story by **Tony Hare**

The Huddlines *noticed an interesting case in a back copy of* The
Metropolitan Police Journal. *It was on the page between the Bribes of the
Month section and the article on 101 Ways of Falling Down The Station Steps.
Apparently, a couple of blokes fell foul of the law, following a street brawl over
a woman. Nothing unusual in that, you might think – except the two men were
eighty-seven and ninety-four respectively and the girlfriend was in her late
eighties. This is their story as recounted by one of them . . .*

My name is Shane Truss. It was late one Saturday night, about 8 o'clock
as I recall, and me and Tracy had just been to a rave at our local disco,
Strangefellows. Never again! The price of the drinks was extortionate and
me on my war pension. Mind you, Trace had enjoyed herself, but then,
she hadn't had to pay for the drinks. When I complained she told me not
to be such a skinflint.

'I enjoyed the last Kneetrembler I had,' she chortled.

'You what!' I expostulated.

'That blue cocktail with the froth on it. Cor what a kick that had.'

'I should think so, at four quid a glass,' I moaned. 'I could've bought three
pairs of trousers in Sue Ryder's for what them drinks cost me.'

I don't think Tracy was listening at this point as she was squinting about
her.

'Ere! Where's Craig?' she asked.

Ah, Craig. The blight of my life, he is. Fancies himself as a bit of a
Lothario. Mind you, the bit in question doesn't work as well as it did.
Even so, he's a right menace down at the Day Centre and he's after my
bint. As always, he'd tagged along with us tonight and now he was
missing. But not for long. As if in answer to Tracy's question – come to

think of it, it *was* in answer to Tracy's question – he emerged, trembling, from the shadows, doing up his fly buttons.

'I'm here!' he announced. 'I 'ad to go in that shop doorway.'

'You dirty bastard!' I expostulated, in my usual eloquent manner.

'No!' said Craig. 'To adjust me appliance! I dislodged it during the lambada.'

'Well, you shouldn't be going in for all that bopping at your age,' Tracy reprimanded him. 'I just enjoyed sitting and listening to the lo-energy music.'

I put in my two-penn'orth. 'I can't understand why you both wanted to come to this dump in the first place. You know Saturday's Gay Nineties night.'

'Well, I misunderstood what it meant,' said Craig.

'Still, you did get that drink bought for you,' Tracy grinned toothlessly at him.

'And an invite back to listen to his Ivor Novello 78s,' I added.

Craig was not amused. 'Shut yer 'ole,' he said. He turned to the light of my life. 'You comin' then, Trace?'

In a jealous rage, I felt the blood crawl to my knees as I saw the red mist. 'Ere, 'ang on, chunky – she's with me.'

'No she's not. I offered her a lift first.'

'I'm not riding on your crossbar again, Craig Stallone,' said Tracy. 'The last time I did that it gave way due to rust.'

'I've had it Kuprinolled,' Craig assured her. 'Anyway, it's faster than his.' He indicated me. I went on the defensive.

'Cobblers!' I muttered in scorn. 'Mine's the latest BMX Mountain Zimmer Frame. So sling yer hook. Go back inside and try and pull one of them bits of old totty who were dancing round their bus-passes.'

But Craig wasn't giving up. 'Tracy – are you coming with me or not?' he pleaded.

Tracy replied, 'If you two are going to argue over me I think it'd be best if I went home on my own.'

'We're not arguing over you,' I said. 'I'll just hang one on him.' I turned to face Craig, my fists clenched threateningly. 'Go on, Craig – put 'em up!'

'You know if I do that I'll fall over,' replied Craig. But he too had the red mist. 'Now be off with you before I fetch you a hefty one up the Khyber with me crutch.'

'A clever trick if you can do it,' I thought. Then I said aloud: 'Right – you've asked for it.' And with that I stamped on his foot with my Doc Marten surgical boot. Craig hopped about in agony before falling over. Surprisingly, for a man of his age, he was back on his feet rather quickly and before I had a chance to be on my guard, he produced the ultimate weapon. One lunge from my assailant and I was in agony, a searing pain racked through my bum.

'Aaaaaargh!' I yelled, clutching my nether regions. 'You swine! You bit me!'

'Yers,' gloated Craig. 'And next time my choppers won't be in my hand – they'll be in my mouth.'

Tracy felt it time she intervened. 'Stop it, you two!' she screamed. 'You're behaving like a couple of yobbos. Don't think you're the only men in my life. I'm off.' She turned to go.

'Ang on, Tracy,' I called after her. 'Where are you going?'

'To see my toy-boy.'

'Toy-boy?' asked Craig, incredulously.

'Yers. And what's more he's famous,' trumped Tracy.

'Blimey! Don't tell me it's Jason Donovan,' said I.

'No, but you're warm,' said she. 'He may say the wrong things now and then, but he knows how to give a girl a good time.'

I couldn't bear the suspense any longer. 'Well, who is it?' I pleaded.

Tracy played her trump card. 'Lord Denning!' she replied. And she hobbled off into the sunset.

A woman who got hooked on sniffing her vacuum cleaner when she was pregnant has just given birth to a baby boy.

Now everytime he crawls into a room people lift their feet up.

Gerry Goddin

Prince Philip uses a pollution-free electric van to drive around London.

That's to compensate for all the lead he puts in the air during the grouse-season.

Oleh Stepaniuk

NO COMPLAINTS
by Richard Stoneman

Scene: A waiting room.

SOUND FX:	*A door creaks open very slowly*
MR H:	*(Soft and gentle)* I'm sorry to bother you. Am I in the right place?
MR T:	*(Timid and slightly moist)* Sorry. I don't know. What are you here for?
MR H:	The lecture on how to complain.
MR T:	Oh, yes – this is the room for that.
MR H:	How do you know?
MR T:	A big man saw me standing in the corridor and told me to sit quietly in here. At least, that was the gist of what he said. I think he was in a bad mood.
MR H:	He wasn't rude to you, was he?
MR T:	Well, yes – actually.
MR H:	I hope you complained to someone.
MR T:	If I could've done that I wouldn't have to be here, would I? *(Slight pause)* Oooooh, sorry. That sounded like I was telling you off.
MR H:	No, no. I'm sorry for being so silly.
SOUND FX:	*Door bangs open*

MS S:	*(Enthusiastic and slightly butch)* Good morning, good morning. It's Mr Humble and Mr Tremble, isn't it? And how are we today?
MR T:	Oh, mustn't grumble.
MR H:	Can't complain.
MS S:	And that's what I'm going to change. My name's Barbara Stoutfellow and I'm here to guide you through my new book: *How To Complain.* Lesson number one – you're in a supermarket. You've just been short-changed at the checkout counter. What do you say, Mr Humble?
MR H:	Um . . . 'Thank you'?
MS S:	No! Mr Tremble?
MR T:	I'd say, 'Where would you like me to leave my trolley?'
MS S:	Stuff your trolley! You must demand your money. Repeat after me, Mr Tremble: 'You owe me one pound fifty'.
MR T:	Do I? I'm so sorry.
MS S:	Not you, you idiot. The checkout girl. All right – forget that. We're in a train now.
MR H:	Is it very crowded?
MS S:	No. Why do you ask?
MR H:	I just wondered if you'd like my seat.
MS S:	Hold on to your seat, Mr Humble. But watch what I'm doing with my hands.
SOUND FX:	*Zip being undone*
MS S:	Can you see what I'm doing, Mr Tremble?
MR T:	Er, yes.

MS S:	And do you like what you see?
MR T:	Er, no.
MS S:	No, you don't. That's because I'm lighting a cigarette, isn't it? And what's that on the window?
MR H:	Oh, don't pigeons make you cross.
MS S:	It's a 'No Smoking' sign! I'm lighting up a Capstan Full Strength in a no smoking compartment. What do you say to me, Mr Tremble?
MR T:	*(Almost firm)* Do you mind . . .
MS S:	*(Goading him on)* That's it . . .
MR T:	*(Firmer)* Do you mind . . .
MS S:	Yes, yes . . .
MR T:	*(Limp)* Do you mind if I open this window?
MS S:	No! You buffoon! Let's try one more exercise. Get up, both of you. Come over here, Mr Tremble. Now you stand right behind him, Mr Humble. A little closer. That's it. Tight behind.
MR H:	Thank you.
MS S:	Can you guess what we're going to do?
MR T:	I hope it's not what I'm thinking.
MS S:	It begins with a 'Q'.
MR T:	I was afraid it might.
MS S:	Queuing, Mr Tremble, You're both queuing and, look – I've pushed in – right in front of you. What are you going to do now?

MR H:	Wait a bit longer to get served?
MS S:	You're going to kick up a fuss. Go on, say what you think of me.
MR H:	You've got very nice hair.
MS S:	*(Screams in frustration)* This is atrocious! You're just a pair of spineless reptiles.
MR T:	Ah, I do have to say something now.
MS S:	At last! What is it, Mr Tremble? Have I gone too far?
MR T:	No. It's just that the definition of a reptile includes being a vertebrate – so it's actually impossible to be a *spineless* reptile.
MS S:	Shut up, you odious little creep. What do I have to do to arouse you? Must I do this?
SOUND FX:	*A very loud slap on the face*
MR T:	Ooooh! You hit me!
MS S:	Yes.
SOUND FX:	*A face slap*
MR H:	You hit him again.
SOUND FX:	*Three more quick face slaps*
MS S:	And I'll go on hitting him until he complains. How about it, Mr Tremble?
	(Pause)
MR T:	I hope you haven't hurt your hand.
MS S:	*(Screams)* That's it! I'm off. You're both hopeless cases.

SOUND FX: *Door slams shut*

MR H: Well, I never. I thought she went too far there. I didn't like to say anything, but . . . really!

MR T: Yes, I must confess I felt something beginning to stir inside me.

MR H: You don't mean . . . ? I wouldn't blame you though. There was no call for physical violence.

MR T: *(Getting excited)* I'm going to go after her.

MR H: You're so bold.

MR T: She only hit me a few times . . .

MR H: Even so, you ought to complain.

MR T: I'm going to. I was just beginning to enjoy it when she stopped. *(Going off shouting)* Come back, Miss Stoutfellow! I think I love you!

STOP PRESS

At an auction this week, a Japanese bought a miniature KGB camera hidden in a jewelled ring.

But all he can do is snap his fingers.

Tony Wheatley

144

STALLONE'S SHAKESPEARIAN AMBITIONS

by Nick R. Thomas

INTERVIEWER: Sylvester Stallone – you've said that your lifelong ambition is to play the lead role in one of Shakespeare's plays. Have you had any offers?

STALLONE: Uh, yeah. I wuz offered *Henry IV Part Two*, but I turned it down.

INTERVIEWER: Why was that? Did you not feel you could do it justice?

STALLONE: Oh no – I just didn't want to appear in yet another sequel.

PARSLEY, SAGE, ROSEMARY AND THYME

by **Alan Whiting**

During most of the Finchley Führer's reign of terror at Number Ten, she was the picture of health. But there was one time when even Mrs T fell victim to a spot of neuralgia. To cure it she didn't bother with the NHS or even Harley Street – no, she finally admitted . . .

MAGGIE: There *is* no alternative!

But there was – alternative medicine, to be precise. Huddlines *hot-footed it to the herbal doctors to see what they prescribed.*

SOUND FX: *Door opening*

MAGGIE: Hello, is this The Hoofer House of Herbalism?

MAURICE: *(Limp of wrist)* Yes – it is, love . . . I'm Maurice the Masseuse. Ooooh, you do look peaky. What's up?

MAGGIE: A pain in the neck.

MAURICE: I know you are, but what's up?

MAGGIE: I've got a touch of neuralgia.

MAURICE: Really? I had a touch of the old one. Ha, ha! Just my little joke. You need a sense of humour in my job.

MAGGIE: So do you in mine. I'm looking for something for my neck.

MAURICE: How about a couple of bolts?

MAGGIE:	No – something herbal. They don't do it on the NHS.
MAURICE:	They don't do *anything* on the NHS these days, dear.
MAGGIE:	Do you know what NHS stands for?
MAURICE:	Of course. No Hospital Staff.
MAGGIE:	No! National Health Service. I can assure you it is safe in my hands.
MAURICE:	That's just what the Boston Strangler said. Look, I'll mix up some oils for a massage. Come on, whip your drawers off.
MAGGIE:	I beg your pardon!
MAURICE:	Off! Whip 'em off! I can't massage you by Osmosis.
MAGGIE:	Disgraceful! I wanted private medicine.
MAURICE:	Private medicine. OK, I'll pull the screens round.
SOUND FX:	*Curtains pulled*
MAURICE:	Everything off, Maggie.
MAGGIE:	*(From behind curtain)* Everything?
MAURICE:	Yes, and your undies.
MAGGIE:	Oh, all right.
SOUND FX:	*Metal objects clanging on floor*
MAGGIE:	There.
MAURICE:	Right – blob yourself down on me palliasse. I've mixed up some oils of Camper.
MAGGIE:	Don't you mean Camphor?
MAURICE:	I know what I mean, love. Now for the massage.

SOUND FX:	*Lots of slapping of skin*
MAURICE:	*(As slapping continues)* Er, Mrs Thatcher . . . ?
MAGGIE:	*(As slapping continues)* Yes?
MAURICE:	*(As slapping continues)* I'm supposed to slap you.
	(Slapping stops)
MAGGIE:	Ooh, you've got cold hands.
MAURICE:	Well, breathe on them for me.
SOUND FX:	*Flamethrower*
MAURICE:	Ta. Mmmm, your skin's very nice. Do you oil it yourself?
MAGGIE:	Why? Should I?
MAURICE:	Well, you don't want it to go rusty. Right, that's the massage – I'll pass you over to a man who's relieved many a throbbing muscle.
SOUND FX:	*Door opening*
MAURICE:	Doctor Friggins!
FRIGGINS:	'Mornin', Mrs T. Here – cop a load of this!
SOUND FX:	*Whoosh*
MAGGIE:	Good Lord! What's that?
FRIGGINS:	All part of the shock treatment. I can get fifteen budgies perched on it now. I hear you've got a stiff one.
MAGGIE:	My neck you mean?
FRIGGINS:	Of course. Herbs are my speciality. In fact, I've just been having a good look at Rosemary round the back.
MAGGIE:	Doctor Friggins – I need some Aromatherapy.

148

FRIGGINS:	Well, missus – I've got lots of aromas. Smell that.
MAGGIE:	*(Sniffs – reacts in disgust)* Yeuuuuuuggghhh!
MAURICE:	What is it?
FRIGGINS:	I don't know, but it's smelt like that for weeks.
SOUND FX:	*Whoosh*
FRIGGINS:	Awww, that's better! Mrs T . . . what you need is plenty of old sage.
MAGGIE:	There's no shortage of that in the House of Lords.
MAURICE:	Yes – and take these potions twice a day. Chervil . . .
FRIGGINS:	*(Handing it to him)* Chervil.
MAURICE:	Borage . . .
FRIGGINS:	Borage.
MAURICE:	Thyme . . . Thyme? . . . Doctor Friggins – have you got the Thyme?
FRIGGINS:	Half past four. Here, anyone want to see my curly endive?
SOUND FX:	*Whoosh*
MAGGIE:	No thank you, doctor. You've both been most helpful. Some people pooh-pooh alternative treatments, but from now on I'll swear by them. Now, if you'll excuse me, I've got to go and see my Financial Adviser and work out our Economic Forecast.
MAURICE:	You mean Nigel Lawson?
MAGGIE:	No – Gypsy Rose Lee. Good day to you.

NB Soon after this event took place we learned that Doctor Friggins was struck off the register – for reasons unknown.

149

STOP PRESS

Glow-in-the-dark condoms are becoming more and more popular.

Well, if the wife's got a headache you can always read in bed.

Gerry Goddin

STOP PRESS

A pensioner has revealed how he made his light bulb last forty years.

It was easy - his electricity was cut off in 1951.

Oleh Stepaniuk

HAPPY BIRTHDAY, NEWS OF THE WORLD

by Tony Hare

SOUND FX:	*Victorian street atmosphere (horses, carriages, crowds etc)*
NARRATOR:	*(John Snagge Type)* London – 1 October 1843, and the cobbles ring out to the sound of clopping horse, rumbling carriage and squelching dog who couldn't get out of the way quick enough. And on every street corner, the cheery newspaper boy selling the latest edition . . .
NEWSBOY:	*(Newsboy)* Read all about it! The *Sunday Filth*! Banana thieves grabbed by the Peelers! Clergyman, Chorister and Organ-pumper in love triangle! Get your copy now! The *Sunday Filth*!
NARRATOR:	Meanwhile, in a building in Holywell Street just off the Strand, a birth is taking place: The *News Of The World*. The first edition is out on the streets and in the editor's office a meeting is taking place.
OMNES:	*(General hubbub)*
EDITOR:	All right, all right, settle down now!
	(They shut up)
EDITOR:	Now that our first edition is out on the streets I have to tell you I am not happy.
WIMPY REPORTER:	Not happy, editor? Why is that?
EDITOR:	Because it's boring, Dempster – that's why. All words. Columns and columns of bleedin' words. Have you seen

151

the *Sunday Filth*? Not only have they got a page three lithograph of some brainless bint showing off her bare ankles . . .

OMNES: *(Gasp of horror)*

EDITOR: Exactly! But they've also scooped a world exclusive royal scandal.

WOMAN: Really? What's that?

EDITOR: I'll tell you what's that, Proops. Only an incident what occurred on the Royal train during a state visit to the slums of Manchester. Allegedly, His Royal Highness, Prince Albert over-imbibed in the dining car and proceeded to moon through the carriage window at well-wishers along the track – much to the chagrin of our beloved Queen. And what story have we come up with? A poxy dispute over the Corn Laws.

WIMPY REPORTER: And why not? That *News Huddlines* gets away with murder.

EDITOR: Never mind the anachronisms, Dempster – next week's edition is going to be vamped up – which is why I've poached two of the *Sunday Filth*'s top newshounds – to give our paper a much needed boost.

WOMAN: Balderdash and Poppycock!

EDITOR: Oh, you've heard of them? Beauregard Balderdash and Ned Poppycock. They'll winkle out a royal scandal if there's one to be winkled out.

WIMPY REPORTER: So where are they?

EDITOR: Out winkling.

NARRATOR: *(Snagge)* Meanwhile – hidden amongst the bushes in the grounds of Buckingham Palace are gentleman tabloid reporter, Beauregard Balderdash, with his colleague, lightning sketch artist, Ned Poppycock.

152

SOUND FX:	*Rustling bushes*
BEAUREGARD:	Come along, Poppycock – there's a good fellow. We've got to get in closer.
NED:	Hang on – I've got my equipment caught in the shrubbery.
BEAUREGARD:	I suppose you *had* to bring your easel with you.
NED:	If you don't want a blurred picture of Queen Victoria, yes. A smudgy etching may be all right for the likes of *Today*, but I take pride in my work.
BEAUREGARD:	Yes, yes – let us proceed with haste. I am sure that is Prince Albert by the gazebo canoodling with Princess Augusta of Cambridge. I'd recognize the beard anywhere.
NED:	I didn't know Princess Augusta had a beard.
BEAUREGARD:	Be quiet, buffoon and have your palette and canvas at the ready. Are you sure you can capture them at this distance?
NED:	Yes, I'll use one of my telephoto paintbrushes. My God – you were right. He's got a woman on his knee and they're smoking out of some strange Eastern-looking vase thing.
BEAUREGARD:	Hookah?
NED:	No, she looks quite respectable to me.
BEAUREGARD:	I'll smack him in the mouth in a minute. What a scoop. The Prince Consort in Opium Orgy. Forget the *News Of The World*. We'll sell this to the highest bidder.
SOUND FX:	*Rustling undergrowth*
VICTORIA:	May we ask what one is doing on our private property?
BEAUREGARD:	Gad! It's Her Majesty! I didn't see you creeping up behind us like that.
VICTORIA:	We have a good mind to set our corgi on one.

BEAUREGARD:	Your Majesty – pray forgive the intrusion. We are but two humble journalists trying to earn an honest crust.
VICTORIA:	Then we must ask one to naff off. This is a gross invasion of our privacy and we are not abused.
BEAUREGARD:	May I quote you on that?
VICTORIA:	One may do as one wishes as long as one scarpers.
BEAUREGARD:	Come along, Poppycock – let us away. I can see the headline now. Queen Victoria says "We are not Abused'. It'll go down in history.
NED:	It'll probably be misquoted.
BEAUREGARD:	Almost certainly, considering the newspaper I intend selling it to.
NED:	You don't mean . . . ?
BEAUREGARD:	Of course – the *Guardian!*

STOP PRESS

A rock star has paid a clinic £8000 to reduce his sex drive.

Blimey, that's a lot of money to pay for a couple of bricks.

Nick R. Thomas

A SIGHT FOR SORE EYES

by **Tony Farrer**

Scene: A pensioner's flat.

ARCHIBALD: *(Roy – an OAP)* Cor – strap up, Mildred! Avert your eyes and keep doing your Aerobics.

MILDRED: *(June – an OAP)* Why – what's up, Archibald?

ARCHIBALD: It's that film star. That Richard Harris geezer. He's standing on his balcony with not a stitch on. He's starkers!

MILDRED: Ooh, Archibald! What can you see?

ARCHIBALD: I can see why he was picked for that film: *A Man Called Horse*!

PAT-A-CAKE, PAT-A-CAKE, BAKER'S MAD

Music: Well-known Nursery Rhymes

New Lyric: JEREMY BROWNE

Kenneth Baker, when he was Minister for Education, revealed that he didn't let his kids watch television because he thought it was rubbish and would corrupt them. He then went on to say that Nursery Rhymes had a far better educational value. The Huddlines *team demonstrated this in their usual tasteful manner:*

ALL: Boys and girls, stay in and work!
There's lots to do, you must not shirk.
If you study and never play,
You might be offered a job one day . . .

ROY: Jack and Jill
Got such a bill
For just one pail of water:
Jack's surprised –
It's privatized!
A hundred quid a quarter!

CHRIS: Nigel Jack Horner
Sat in a corner
Peeling his Budget plums:
He stood in his suit,
And pulled out a fruit,
And said 'These are all for *my chums*!'

JUNE: Cecil Pecil, what a good egg,
Kissed a girl and made her preg.;
Then, because he was a toff,
Cecil Pecil just pushed off.

CHRIS/ROY: Hey diddle diddle
We're all on the fiddle,
We all like plenty of fun:
ROY: But nobody wants
His name in print
When the dish sells her tale to the *Sun*.

JUNE: Little boy blue,
Go sweep up the wool,
The lamb's in a mountain,
The quota is full.
ROY: We do not care
What you paid for the sheep:
They're in a big freezer,
Going cheap.

CHRIS: Mary, Mary, quite contrary,
How does your garden grow?
JUNE: With acid rain,
And *our* food chain,
I really am blessed if I know . . .

ROY: Tom, Tom, the pauper's lad
Stole a pig for his starving dad:
The pig was fried,
But poor Dad died,
And Tom got eighteen months inside!

JUNE: See-Saw, Margery Daw,
Johnny's not frightfully brainy:
He shall have but a penny a day,
Because he's a YTS trainee.

ALL: Saatchi Waatchi sat on his bot:
Margy Wargy liked him a lot:
She paid him more than she paid other men,
Cos he made the punters elect her again.

157

STOP PRESS

A thief has been caught stealing bras from a women's R.A.F. base.

He told the police he was just having a look around the 'hangars'.

Nick R. Thomas

STOP PRESS

A survey found that 1 in 5. women would rather do their shopping than have sex.

And the other 4 can't go into Tescos any more.

Tony Wheatley